I0119492

Anonymous

The British Empire League

Meeting at Guildhall, London, December 3rd, 1896

Anonymous

The British Empire League
Meeting at Guildhall, London, December 3rd, 1896

ISBN/EAN: 9783337164645

Printed in Europe, USA, Canada, Australia, Japan

Cover: Foto ©Suzi / pixelio.de

More available books at **www.hansebooks.com**

Devonshire

BRITISH EMPIRE LEAGUE.

MEETING AT THE GUILDHALL, LONDON,

December 3rd, 1896.

MEETING of the League was held at the Guildhall, London, on Thursday, December 3rd, 1896, the Right Hon. the Lord Mayor, who attended in state, presiding. There was a large attendance ; among those on the platform and in the body of the hall being His Grace the Duke of Devonshire, K.G. (the President of the League), the Right Hon. Sir John Lubbock, Bart., M.P. (Hon. Treasurer), Sir Robert Herbert, G.C.B. (Chairman of Executive), W. Herbert Daw (acting Hon. Treasurer), the Hon. Sir Charles Tupper, Bart., G.C.M.G., C.B. (M.P., Canada), Sir Westby Perceval, K.C.M.G., the Hon. R. R. Dobell (M.P., Canada), the Hon. Alban Gibbs, M.P., Sir T. Sutherland, K.C.M.G., M.P., Sir Howard Vincent, M.P., Right Hon. Admiral Sir John Dalrymple Hay, K.C.B., Sir Frederick Young, K.C.M.G., General Laurie, M.P., B. H. Cohen, M.P., Matthew Wallace (the Chief Commoner), G. N. Hooper, W. Becket Hill, Colonel Innes, Dr. W. Culver James, Herman W. Marcus, Lieut.-General Sir Andrew Clarke, R.E., G.C.M.G., C.B., C.I.E., G. Drage, M.P., F. Wootton-Isaacson, M.P., Viscount Sidmouth, Sir Henry Mance, Colonel Welby, M.P., Viscount de Vesci, General Sir Richard Harrison, K.C.B., Sir Rivers Wilson, C.B., Captain H. M. Jessel, M.P., Justice Danavall, R. Cavendish, M.P., H. Trengrouse, Howard

Morley, Admiral Boys, Sir Thomas Storey, General Wardell, Sir Ambrose Shea, K.C.M.G., and C. Freeman Murray (Secretary).

The Lord Mayor, who was cordially received, in opening the proceedings, said : I call on the Secretary to read a letter.

The Secretary : I have this morning received a letter from the Secretary of the League in Canada, which I think it is important to read. The letter was as follows :—

10 EQUITY CHAMBERS,
ADELAIDE STREET EAST,
TORONTO.

DEAR SIR, *November* 19*th*, 1896.

In pursuance of the request of the League in England, the Canadian Branch have elected ten members of the Council of the League in England, whose names and addresses are as follow:--Sir Donald Smith, K.C.M.G., London, Sandford Fleming, Esq., C.M.G., Ottawa, G. R. Parkin, Esq., M.A., Toronto, Lieut.-Colonel G. T. Denison, Toronto, J. M. Clark, Esq., Toronto, D'Alton McCarthy, Esq., Q.C., M.P., Toronto, A. McNeill, Esq., M.P., Toronto, J. Castell Hopkins, Esq., Toronto, J. T. Small, Esq., Toronto, and J. Herbert Mason, Esq. Toronto. I have much pleasure in enclosing you sterling draft for £10 10s., being the membership fee of the ten gentlemen above mentioned. I have the honour to be

Yours faithfully,

GEORGE E. EVANS,
Hon. Sec.

C. Freeman Murray, Esq.,
    Botolph House, Eastcheap, E.C.

THE LORD MAYOR:

My Lord, Ladies and Gentlemen,—Whenever there is a meeting of any sort it is the usual custom for someone to take the chair. In the City of London it is the privilege of the Lord Mayor, whenever he attends a meeting, to do so—(hear, hear)—but it is not necessary that he should either make a speech, or be in any way answerable for whatever is said—(laughter). I am proud to-day that it is my prerogative to take the chair, and I am particularly glad because the object of it is entirely in harmony with my own views and sentiments—(cheers). Although I have said that it is not necessary for the Chief Magistrate to intrude any of his personal observations, yet I am going, with your permission, to avail myself of my position, by taking up your time for a few moments, and for a few moments only, to tell you what I venture to think of this great and important occasion. I am emboldened to do so because I am the Chief Magistrate of this City, and in that capacity I represent the large commercial interests of the City—(cheers). I make bold to do so because I have the honour of having been connected with a firm for the past thirty-five years who have had considerable transactions in every part of the globe, and I am gratified to find that this fact has been acknowledged, both in my person as Chief Magistrate and as a member of the firm, by a visit from the Consuls, who were good enough to present me with an address signed in the first place by the Austrian Consul, Mr. Alfred Rothschild. The City is indeed a fit and proper place where a meeting such as this should be held —(hear and cheers)—because I would point out that commerce is the keystone of that remarkable edifice, our great Empire. Sanguinary wars have been fought from time immemorial—sanguinary wars have been fought even within our own memories—for the acquisition of territory, and in each and every instance it seems to me that the primary cause of the acquisition of territory is to promote the interests of commerce, and therefore the proper place for a meeting such as this is the Guildhall of the City of London—(cheers). Many subjects in connection with this meeting will have to be discussed at a future date, but I think we should primarily come to some conclusion. When men assemble round a table to play some game they do not commence dealing out the "fish," or come to a unanimous decision what stakes they shall play for, but they frame the principles and rules of the game before they commence; and so I venture to say that before we discuss fiscal arrangements, tariffs, boundaries, and various most important questions, we should first come to some distinct unanimous conclusion that would meet the approval of the Empire at large—(hear, hear). "Our Colonies," I know, is a very favourite term, but "Our Colonies" is an expression which I think should pass away. Our Colonies are as much related to this great Empire as the hands, the arms, and the head of a body are related to a human being. And what constitutes a perfect man, as far as anything human can be perfect? It is that each one of his limbs should be in perfect health and in possession of full strength; and so this Empire will be a perfect Empire when each and every portion of it is strong, because the strength of each portion means the strength of the whole, and the weakness of any one portion, however remote, seriously affects the whole body. We have community of interests; we must have community of obligations—(cheers). Empires have flourished and empires have failed, and the primary cause, no doubt, of the collapse of an empire is that the empire produced nothing. The second cause, no doubt, lay in the fact of its degeneracy, its effeminacy, and the maladministration of its colonies; but there is, in my humble opinion, one other reason. The Romans were perfectly well aware of the great value of roads. No better road-makers have ever existed since that time; but they did

G. Fauden Philip

not sufficiently recognise the great importance of rapid inter-communication, and they lost their possessions before they knew how badly they were administered, and the enemy was at their gates before they had any knowledge of his proximity. The insular position of Great Britain has made it what it is. Its mastery of the sea will, I hope, always be maintained—(hear, hear). It must be if we wish to maintain our Empire, our greatness, and our commerce. Ladies and gentlemen, the Mansion House is the home of many schemes and many suggestions. I would venture to think that perchance as fitting a manner as any of celebrating her most Gracious Majesty's sixtieth anniversary—(cheers)—would be to lay at the feet of that great Lady—who is not only the first lady in England, but the first lady in the world—a scheme for the absolute and perfect unification of this great Empire—(cheers). Ladies and gentlemen, I will only detain you for one single moment longer. Our ships which go backwards and forwards to the various Colonies which are part and parcel of our Empire—bearing with them freight from this country, and bringing back freight from our other possessions, carrying with them messages of peace, goodwill, and encouragement, and bringing back answers that we gladly welcome—are like the shuttles in the hands of the weaver. Each ship as it goes backwards and forwards takes a thread, here, there, and everywhere, and brings it back again till, bit by bit, a fabric is woven and consolidated which makes this great Empire what it is—(cheers). I will now ask the Duke of Devonshire to move the first resolution.

The Duke of Devonshire :

My Lord Mayor, Ladies and Gentlemen,—I have been asked to move the first of the resolutions which are to be proposed to you at this meeting. It is a very short one, and I will read it at once. The resolution is : " That this meeting cordially approves the constitution of the British Empire League, and learns with satisfaction that its organisation is now complete, and that it is in a position to take up in due order the important subjects set forth in its programme." Ladies and gentlemen, I must begin by offering a few words of explanation, and, I am afraid, of excuse, for my appearance in the capacity of President of this League. It is a position for which I possess but very few qualifications. I have not had the opportunity of personally visiting and making myself acquainted with any of our great Colonies. It is now, I am afraid, almost thirty-three years ago since I paid the only visit which I have paid to one of our colonies—the Canadian Provinces, as they were at that time—and I need not remind you that both the Government and the development of the Canadian Provinces were at that period a very different thing from what they have since become. Neither have I had, in the numerous official positions I have had the honour to hold, any connection with the Colonial Office. I must confess that I have not paid any special attention to Colonial political questions, and that others have occupied a great deal more of my attention. For these reasons I have felt a very considerable reluctance in accepting the post of President of this League, and I think that if it had not been for the very persistent pressure which was placed upon me by my friend Sir John Lubbock, who is here to-day—(cheers)—I should probably never have made up my mind to accept that office. I have not yet come to the end of my excuses. I was unable to be present at the inaugural meeting of this League, which was held in London last year, and the executive body of the League have been, perhaps, somewhat remiss in reminding me of my duties as President, and I have but a very imperfect acquaintance with practical proceedings which have since that time been taken by those who have had the direction of its operations. Now, gentlemen, these explanations and excuses—necessary, I think, to account for the many shortcomings which I fear you will find in what I have to state to you—may perhaps prepare you for the further admission I am about to make : that in taking part in these proceedings to-day I am not going to represent to you that we are making any great and momentous new departure, fraught with far-reaching consequences to our Colonies or ourselves. Experience has, I think, taught those who have this cause in hand the necessity of caution, of moderation, of patience, and perhaps even of humility—(hear, hear). I believe that the idea of Imperial Unity as a sentiment, as an aspiration—perhaps, as it has often been described, as a dream—is one which has made progress and continues to make progress in the minds and convictions of men both at home and in the Colonies—(hear, hear)—but as a practical movement, as a movement in the direction of effecting great constitutional changes, of bringing about large alterations in the official connection between Great Britain and her Colonies—as a movement in the direction of bringing about a greater commercial unity between the different portions of the Empire—it must be admitted that those who have been engaged in this movement have experienced some checks, and that some enthusiastic anticipations which have been formed have been in some degree disappointed, and one of these checks has been no doubt the dissolution of the Imperial Federation League, which was the predecessor of that which we have now formed. That League had its primary object, among others, of bringing about some form of confederation between Great Britain and her Colonies, and it must be admitted that as a practical movement the

object with which that federation was formed has not yet
been attained, and that no great progress in that direction
has yet been made. I should have liked if time had permitted
to have said something to you on the subject of Colonial
history, and of the influence which that history had upon the
history of our country. I should have liked to have been
able to say something to you upon the nature of the idea
of Imperial Unity, and the practical as well as the sentimental considerations which have turned the minds of
many men in that direction ; but I have to remember that
I am not addressing an ordinary political meeting, but I am
addressing men whose time is valuable, and that we are
assembled not for the purpose of indulging in flights of
oratory, but for a practical purpose of immediate importance.
All these things I take for granted, and I do so with the more
readiness because I know that the general considerations
affecting this question have often in this hall been described
by those who are far better qualified than I am to speak on
this subject. I take these things for granted, therefore,
and I will only state as an undoubted fact that, striking as
our Colonial history in the past has been ; large as is the
part which that history must always take in the history of
the world itself; there is in the opinion of many men a still
greater future in store for Great Britain and her Colonies,
and that England—when I speak of England of course I
mean the United Kingdom—may not only in the future
become, as she has been in the past, the greatest centre of
colonising energy, but that we may in the future be able to
avoid the errors of the past, to escape from those influences,
obstacles and hindrances which have impeded unity and
tended to disruption, and that England may become not
only the mother and founder of great and independent
States, but that she and they may grow up together in one
still greater and more powerful community—(cheers).
These are ideas, these are aspirations, not only of speculative
enthusiasts, but which have been held by practical
politicians. The Imperial Federation League was founded to

carry out the idea of Imperial Unity. It has been presided over, and its proceedings have been guided, by practical statesmen, such as the late Mr. Forster—(cheers)—Lord Rosebery—(cheers)—and the late Mr. Stanhope. Others who have not been directly connected with the Federation League have warmly sympathised in its objects. The present Prime Minister—(cheers)—described the subject brought before him by a deputation from that League as one involving neither more nor less than the future of the British Empire. Mr. Chamberlain—(cheers)—the present Secretary of the Colonies, has never concealed his sympathy with the objects of the late Federation League. That League did a great deal to call public attention to this question, and to bring it home to the minds of men both in the Colonies and at home. The most important step which has ever been taken in the direction of Imperial Unity was in some degree owing to the exertions of the late Imperial Federation League. When, in the year 1887, a conference met in London, presided over by Imperial statesmen, attended by the most prominent men from all our Colonies, which discussed and arrived at practical conclusions on a large number of subjects of common interest, it almost justified, if it did not completely justify, the declaration which was made respecting it by Lord Rosebery—that the mere assembling and deliberations of that conference had brought about the commencement of Imperial Federation. Un-happily that conference has not been followed, as it was hoped might have been the case, by others of the same character, and with the exception of that which was held a few years ago at Ottawa — which not meeting at the centre of the Empire, of course attracted less attention, and, perhaps, gave less importance to its deliberations—those Colonial conferences have not been since repeated, and in the steps which have been taken since 1887 with the object of accelerating and com-pleting the work which was begun, another of those checks I have referred to has been met with by the advocates of this cause. In response to an invitation of Lord Salisbury the late Federation League undertook to prepare the outlines of a scheme of confederation which it was hoped might form the subject of discussion at another conference. As it turned out, that enterprise was one of too ambitious a character. No action followed upon the preparation of that scheme, and partly, I think, in consequence of differences of opinion which arose within the League in regard to it, partly from other causes into which it is not necessary that I should now enter, the preparation of that scheme was shortly followed by the dissolution, by its own act, of the Imperial Federation League. Some of its members, however, declined to accept the rebuff or the reverse which they had thus sustained. Some of them thought that a great blow would be struck at the cause of Imperial Unity if the work on which that League had been engaged should be entirely suspended, and while they recognised that its importance must in some degree be modified, while it became necessary that its objects should be of a less ambitious character—a less ambitious or daring character—it was thought that the duty of informing and educating the public mind, which had been usefully and successfully undertaken by the League, might still be continued, and that was the purpose with which this British Empire League had been constituted, with the object of continuing the operations of the late League—of its predecessor—so far as they have been of value, and it is hoped that this humbler aim may at least have the effect of preparing the way for the consideration of larger plans, which in the opinion of some are still within the possibility of realisation. Now, my Lord Mayor, this is a matter which, in our opinion, is one upon which you and the citizens of London are capable of rendering great service—(cheers). I suppose there is no body of men within the Empire who are more deeply interested in the closer connection between Great Britain and her Colonies than citizens and merchants, and the commercial men of

London—(cheers). You will probably all agree with Mr. Chamberlain when he said, a few months ago, that if we intended to approach this question of Imperial Unity in a practical spirit it must be approached from its commercial side—(hear, hear, and cheers). On that occasion he did not, as I think he has been erroneously represented to have done, make any proposals upon the subject of commercial unity. What he did was to point out that the proposals and suggestions in the direction of commercial union, which had hitherto been made at the Conferences at Ottawa and elsewhere, did not offer a sufficient *quid pro quo*, that the advantages which were offered were not sufficient to induce this country to incur the certain loss, and to take the possible risk of revising altogether her commercial policy. What he did was to follow the suggestion contained in a despatch of his predecessor, Lord Ripon, and to point out that another proposal—a proposal involving free trade within the Empire, although such a principle might derogate from the strict principles of free trade—might, if it were made by the Colonies, be a proper subject for discussion, and might be discussed at another Colonial Conference. That was the suggestion, not the proposal, which was made by Mr. Chamberlain, but it must be acknowledged—and here I come again to one of the checks which those who have this cause at heart have sustained—that that suggestion has not hitherto met with any such response from our principal Colonies as would justify its becoming the subject of discussion at another Conference, and probably we must admit that the time is not yet ripe for the discussion either of commercial proposals which were made at the Conference at Ottawa or of that other proposal which Lord Ripon and Mr. Chamberlain suggested might properly become a subject of discussion between ourselves and the Colonies. But, my lords and gentlemen, although the time may not be ripe for the discussion of such large questions as these, there must be many points connected with the

great subject on which it is possible that those who are
carrying on the trade between England and her Colonies
might be capable of making suggestions which would lead
to a better understanding between our Government and
Colonial Governments upon many matters affecting their
and our commercial interests ; and it might be possible—I
think it would be possible—for the merchants of London—
for those who are engaged in the trade of London and
the Colonies—to make suggestions of an informal character,
through the agency of such an association as this, which
would pave the way for the formation of such a
better understanding—(cheers)—and it might be possible
for them to collect materials which would form the
basis of discussion at another conference which might be
held on the subject. But I feel that these are matters
upon which many of those on this platform are far more
capable of speaking than I am, and with your permission
I shall leave this branch of the subject entirely to them.
There is, however, one subject which was discussed at the
Colonial Conference of 1887, which has in my opinion again
become a subject of practical and almost immediate importance. I have referred to the great moral effect which was
produced by that conference as a visible symbol of the
Empire—(cheers)—but in addition to that it had, at least,
one immediate result of a practical character. The
Naval Agreement which was entered into between this
Country and the Australian Colonies and the Colony
of New Zealand was the outcome of that conference.
By that agreement, the Colonies undertook to pay
the interest on the cost of construction, and a part
of the cost of maintenance of a considerable addition to
our fleet, to be maintained in Australian waters for the
protection of British and Colonial commerce—(cheers).
Those Colonies had already undertaken considerable
obligations of a naval and military character for their own
defence, but this agreement was the first recognition which
had ever been made by any of the Colonies of the duty

and interests of the Colonies to contribute to the support
of the Imperial Navy—(cheers). The term during which
that arrangement will last will very soon approach its
conclusion, and it will be for the parties concerned to
decide whether that agreement should be allowed to lapse
or whether it should be renewed. I may say that Her
Majesty's present Government attach the greatest importance to a renewal in some form or other of that agreement
—(cheers). The terms are, of course, open to consideration,
but that it should be renewed is a subject which, in our
opinion, is of the highest importance, not only on account
of the pecuniary considerations involved; not only on
account of the actual addition to our naval forces which it
provides; but also as a step towards a practical measure of
federation for the purposes of defence—a measure of
federation which, with the growth of our Colonies, may
make available for Imperial defence the whole resources,
both of the British Empire and of her Colonies—(cheers).
I have found with very great satisfaction on my return to
office, after an absence from official life of a good·many
years, the large progress which has been made in the
consideration of the great question of Imperial defence.
A body is now in existence—has been for many years in
existence—called the Colonial Defence Committee, composed of representatives of the Admiralty, the War Office,
and the Colonial Office; that body has made a complete
study of the question of Colonial defence as it affects
every Colony of the British Empire. It has studied the
question from the point of view of each colony; and
every colony, whether it be a Crown Colony or a self-
governing colony, is now in possession of the views of
Her Majesty's Government as to the nature of the attack—
the possible attack—to which any of them may be exposed,
and as to the means of defence which it is possible to
oppose to such attack. Every Colonial Government now
knows what the Imperial Government is prepared to undertake in their defence, and what must be left to themselves

to undertake. Now, although the instructions to this committee, and the plans which this committee has prepared, are, and must be, to a very great extent, of a confidential character, yet I am permitted to make a public announcement of the principles upon which those plans are based; so that not only the public at home but everyone of our Colonial fellow-subjects should know how much. it is that the Government are prepared to undertake in the defence of the Colonies, and the duties which in their turn they think ought to be undertaken by the Colonies themselves. These principles are as follows :— The maintenance of sea supremacy has been assumed as the basis of the system of Imperial defence against attack from over the sea. This is the determining factor in shaping the whole defensive policy of the Empire, and is fully recognised by the Admiralty, who have accepted the responsibility of protecting all British territory abroad against organised invasion from the sea. To fulfil this great charge they claim the absolute power of disposing of their forces in the manner they consider most certain to secure success, and object to limit the action of any part of them to the immediate neighbourhood of places which they consider may be more effectively protected by operations at a distance. It is recognised, however, that Her Majesty's ships, engaged in hunting out and destroying the squadrons of an enemy, may not be in a position to prevent the predatory raids of hostile cruisers on British ports. The strength of such an attack will vary in the different parts of the world according to the strength of possibly hostile navies, the proximity of their bases, and the troops that are or could easily be brought there in anticipation of war. It also varies from time to time with changing political combinations. But it is improbable that this raiding attack would be made by more than a few ships, nor could it be of any permanent effect unless troops could be landed. In no case could a greater force than a few thousand men be collected and conveyed without such arrangements and preparation as would bring the operations under the category of those which the Navy has undertaken to prevent. Against a raid of the nature indicated, it has been considered necessary to make secure those places which are essential to the Navy for coaling, refitting, and repairing. Ports for this purpose have been selected by the Admiralty, and Imperial resources in men and money available for use abroad have been concentrated on their defence. Apart from the harbours fortified for the Navy, there are other ports which, though they do not enter into what may be called the general strategic scheme, are also liable from their commercial importance to predatory raids, and which require measures of defence for the protection of the special interests involved. The resources of places which, in the opinion of an enemy, would justify the very considerable risks which a raid on them would involve are generally sufficient to admit of the provision of local defence by local means ; and where the liability to attack and the resources to resist attack co-exist it has been held to be the duty of the colony to make provision for adequate defence. In dealing with places of this nature the Committee have advocated the creation of sufficient fixed defences to prevent their unmolested occupation by hostile cruisers, but more especially the provision of troops sufficient to deal effectually with such forces as an enemy must put on shore to enable him to secure any permanent advantage from his attack. Troops without works may defeat an enemy and frustrate his object ; works without troops are useless and delusive. It is necessary to lay stress on this fact, as fortifications give an appearance and feeling of security which is not justified unless they are fully garrisoned by well-trained men and supported by mobile forces, and because expenditure on defences involving a heavy outlay at one time and little at another can be more easily fitted into the exigencies of fluctuating budgets than expenditure on troops, which must be constant to be effective. When money is made available in time of

anticipated war, there is a tendency to spend it in increasing
fortifications and armaments, sometimes already on an unne-
cessarily elaborate and extensive scale, while in time of external
quiet and internal financial depression there is a tendency to
reduce to a dangerous extent the military forces which can
only be of value if constantly kept up to a state of efficiency
in numbers and training. I think in these few paragraphs
that the principles of Colonial defence have been stated with
a clearness which leaves nothing to be desired. The obligations which the Imperial Government is prepared to
undertake in the defence of her Colonies as well as of herself,
and those which the Colonies are expected to undertake in
their own defence, have been clearly defined. And now I trust
that these principles having been clearly stated, these mutual
obligations being clearly understood—both by the Imperial
Government and the Colonial Governments—when the
time comes, as I trust it shortly will come, when another
Conference will be held—(hear, hear)—for the purpose of
considering, and, I trust, renewing, the naval arrangement
with the Australasian and, I hope, with the other Colonies,
the same opportunity will be taken of rediscussing the
whole question of Colonial defence. Now, therefore, that
the principles have been clearly established, and the
British people, at the instance of their Government, have
taken on themselves vast obligations in order to strengthen
their fleet and to enable it to fulfil its responsibilities—not
only to our own country, but also to the Colonies—I trust
the Colonies themselves, stimulated by the example which
has been set by some, will not hesitate to do all that is
necessary to discharge what I think is the very moderate
share of those duties which it is proposed to impose upon
them. Ladies and gentlemen, it is for the discussion and
consideration of, and for furnishing and providing knowledge and information upon, subjects such as these that the
British Empire League has been founded and ventures to
think it may be of some service. As at present constituted,
it does not undertake to frame constitutions, or to elaborate

Alban Gibbs

commercial systems. Its more modest, but I think still useful, aim is to furnish a channel of communication between Englishmen at home and Englishmen abroad —(cheers)—to discuss difficulties, and, it may be, to remove misunderstandings, which still stand in the way of a complete Imperial Unity ; and I think that if we can discharge this important though not ambitious object the League will not have deserved badly of the citizens of London, or of the inhabitants of this great country as a whole—(cheers). To lead the people of this country and of the Colonies to a better understanding and knowledge of the various elements of the questions of commercial unity and of general defence—these are objects which, in its present constitution, this League sets before you, and I trust that by approving this resolution you will give your sanction to the constitution and formation of the League—(loud cheers).

Mr. Alban Gibbs, M.P. :

After the most eloquent speech which you have just heard from your President, it would not become me to do more than formally second the resolution. You heard from your President how this League rose, Phœnix-like, from the ashes of a former League, hardly a year ago, under the name of the British Empire League. I myself think that that is a better name than that of the Imperial Federation League, because our present name binds us to no exact method by which to gain our ends, although it does bind us very clearly to certain most important principles. It is true, as the Duke of Devonshire has said, that some of those principles are not new, but they are none the less important, and it is none the less necessary to insist on them time after time. For one thing, we are bound not to be Little Englanders ; for another thing, every member of this League has adopted the principle—the very old principle—that union is strength, and in adopting that he also adopts the necessity of keeping up the union which most happily exists between us and our Colonies, as that is the best union we can possibly have. I think, too, that a member of this League regards the independence of the Empire.— the building up of commerce on a firm basis, and making it not dependent on other nations—as even more important than occasionally buying something at less than it costs to produce. I do not think I should detain you further. The Duke of Devonshire has said everything that can be said about our objects, but there is one sentence which fell from Mr. Chamberlain in his speech which has so happily expressed our objects that I should like to read it. "To organise an empire—you may almost say to create an empire—greater and more potent for peace and the civilisation of the world than any history has ever known—that is a dream, if you like ; but it is a dream of which no man need be ashamed "—(cheers). This British Empire League is established to make that dream a reality, and that being so, I ask you to pass this resolution with that unanimity which it deserves both for itself and for the way the Duke of Devonshire proposed it.

The LORD MAYOR put the motion to the meeting in the usual way, and declared it carried.

MR. DOBELL :

My Lord Mayor, Ladies and Gentlemen,—In moving the resolution which I have had placed in my hands
to-day, I may say that it would give me intense gratification
if I should be able to say anything that might tend to the
advancement of this League. Persons of all shades of
politics, and leaders of the two great parties—men justly
regarded as our leaders—have from time to time reiterated
the great desire they have for a more united and closer bond
between Great Britain and her Colonies. For myself, I have
always thought that the first actual scheme which was laid down
by the late and much-lamented Right Honourable W. E.
Forster, in his essay pointing out the aims of Imperial Federation, contained almost everything that we have to strive
for to-day. The difficulty is that while nearly everyone
accepts the principles which he enunciated in that essay, we
find it so difficult to make any advance in the practical
progress of carrying out the scheme. Our executive committee have had to keep our rank and file merely moving by
the "goose-step," making no progress. We have held
conferences ; we have listened to eminent politicians who
have spoken advocating the interests of this League ; we
have heard some advocate Imperial defence, while others
have contended that the one great necessity for Imperial
Federation is to have discriminating duties between Great
Britain and her Colonies—in other words, a Zollverein
including Great Britain and her Colonies as against the
world—(cheers). Notwithstanding all these efforts, we meet
to-day after sixteen years of work, for, my Lord, it is just a
little past sixteen years since a deputation authorised by the
representation of Colonial visitors in this city, and joined
by members of the Associated Chambers of Commerce,
waited upon your Grace and the Right Hon. Lord Kimberley,
and we then advocated and urged strongly a change in the
fiscal policy of this country in favour of discriminating duties

to aid federation. Well, I think in all fairness it is only right to-day to say that many of us who then expressed views would pause before we spoke quite as strongly if we had to take part in such a deputation again to-morrow. This country stands to-day "splendidly isolated," if you like, but with a record of having followed the noblest and possibly the wisest course, discarding all attempts at a retaliatory policy, continuing on her course of what many call "one-sided free trade," but offering to the world an example of proud independence and the highest example of unselfish trade principles—(cheers). Is there any other country in the world to-day with a population so numerous, deriving her supplies very largely from the outer world, and still enjoying the same measure of prosperity and comfort? And as regards the Colonies outside Great Britain herself, is there any other country which has extended to them the same measure of freedom we enjoy, and not only we, as one of the self-governing Colonies, but the Crown Colonies? Where do we find in the Colonies of any other European Power that they have been granted the same extent of freedom and independence as has been extended, through the generosity of Great Britain, to self-governing Colonies belonging to this country?—(cheers). The greatest misfortune that could possibly happen to any territory over which this country has at any one time ex-tended her Protectorate has been when, for some State reasons we know little of, she has been induced to withdraw her Protectorate and leave that territory in the hands of some other country. I cannot help recalling what Sheridan put into the mouth of that Peruvian who, in reply to an offer made by the invaders of his country, said this, "They offer us their protection! Such protection as vultures give to lambs, covering and devouring them!" But that is not the case with England. Look throughout the world to-day and see what Great Britain has accomplished. For myself, I am happy to belong to the Dominion of Canada —a country that I do not think to-day is second to any in

Richd R. Dobell

its boundless resources, in its general prosperity, and, above all, in its real, earnest, and lively loyalty to this Mother Country—(loud cheers). I should like to say a word or two about our near neighbour, the great United States. We cannot help looking with admiration at the wonderful success of those States, but we have a greater admiration than that, and that is to look to this country, and see the forbearance and generosity which she has shown to the United States for the last twenty-five years. For myself, I have very great hopes that that forbearance and generosity will not be thrown away—that we are nearing the time when the United States will realise to some extent what has been done for her. I do not wish to speak disparagingly of the United States, but I do point out the working of her navigation laws, her alien laws, and the arrangements about her canals, and contrast them with those of Great Britain. Probably very few of you know much of the arrangements that were made between Canada and the United States in the year 1869. Great Britain made a treaty with the United States, giving to the United States the use of our rivers and canals on the same terms as we use those canals ourselves. This year alone through the Sault Ste. Marie Canal four million tons of shipping came free, belonging to the United States. On the other hand, the United States under that treaty promised that they would use their best endeavours to obtain from several sovereign States the same privileges for Canada. Well, our boats leaving Canada and wishing to go to New York are stopped at Albany. They can go no further because there is a twelve-mile canal. On the other hand, the Americans can leave New York and come up to Canada, using our canals and rivers, and going back free, without hindrance. I do not name this as a grievance, because it is not of much moment, but it is one of the many little things which are not appreciated in this country, which we in Canada have had to bear with. However, as I said before, I

believe that the time is coming when we shall have a better
state of things with the United States. I am not so sure
that Canada will not be the instrument of bringing about a
much better understanding ; and I am quite sure that, if she
is able to do it, the effort will be recognised by this country
as one of the best things Canada ever did or could do for
the Mother Country. I have only said this much as speaking
of the views we have in Canada. I have not said it to discourage, but to stimulate the members of the British Federation League. I believe myself—and I said fifteen years ago
that it would take fifteen years before this would become a
practical question—I believe that to-day it is growing all over
the country. It is growing rapidly in Canada, and they are
urging us to make further advances than we have made. I
cannot help alluding to an eminent writer whom you all know,
Mr. Goldwin Smith, who anticipates that the goal of Canada
will be that it will be absorbed into the United States. Now
here is one practical good to be derived from Imperial
Federation. If we join and become one in this federation
we may possibly be able to take in the United States—
(laughter)—and I am sure that we should all be very
pleased to have our erring cousin back again—(cheers).
Without taking up more of your time, I beg to move :—

> "That the President, Vice-Presidents, Executive
> Officers, and Council, as shown on printed list, be
> elected for the ensuing year, with power to add to their
> number."

C

SIR WESTBY PERCEVAL:

My Lord Mayor, Ladies, and Gentlemen,—I have very great pleasure indeed in seconding this resolution. Mr. Dobell, in proposing the resolution, told us something of the opinions prevailing in Canada with respect to cementing the relationship between the Mother Country and the Dominion; and as one hailing from Australasia I am happy to be able to say that we on the other side of the world are not one whit the less earnest in our desire to promote this closer relationship than are the people of Canada. I know that many people think that the cause of Imperial unity has during recent years sustained a severe check—in fact, our President to-day has referred to many of these checks; and I thought that I noticed a ring of disappointment in his utterances in that regard. We are all disappointed, it is true, that the cause has not made more rapid progress, but for my own part I think it is a matter for the very greatest congratulation that so much has been done during the last ten or fifteen years. If we go back in our minds and compare public opinion at that time, both here and in the Colonies, with public opinion as evinced to-day, we see that a very great deal of progress has been made. The Duke has pointed to one practical result of the last conference—the establishment of the Australasian Squadron. We have, moreover, sitting to-day a Royal Commission to enquire into a scheme for the Pacific cable, the object of which is to bring into closer communication the Australasian and Canadian Colonies— (cheers). I see too in this morning's papers that a resolution was passed yesterday in the Legislative Assembly of Victoria urging that an Imperial Conference should be held to discuss the important question of commercial union—(cheers). We all know the many difficulties which beset this problem; but those difficulties, to my mind, are the most fascinating part of it, because I think that Englishmen

C 2

rejoice in tackling a project which is beset with difficulties, and, given the desire, I cannot help thinking that some way will be found to overcome these difficulties. As City merchants, you know that the trade between this country and foreign countries is larger in volume than the trade between this country and the Colonies, and you naturally and very properly hesitate to jeopardise that foreign trade; but the trade with the Colonies is fast over-hauling the trade which this country does with foreign countries, and when those two volumes of trade approximate, or the position is reversed and the Colonial trade is of more value to this country than the foreign trade, then the time will be ripe for the completion of a scheme for Customs' Union. I have the greatest hope, however, that even before that time comes considerable progress will be made with the details of the plan for carrying out this great object. I heard the Lord Mayor, in his opening remarks, make a suggestion that we could not offer a better memorial to Her Majesty during this coming year than to lay at her feet a complete scheme for Imperial Unity. Would that we might be able to do so! I fear very much that the time has not yet come for that, but, short of a scheme of Imperial Unity, we will be able to give to Her Majesty most gratifying evidence of the loyal affections of her subjects all over the globe and the most positive assurances of their desire to work together for the advancement of her Empire as a whole. I will not take up your time any longer. I think the objects of the League can be endorsed by everyone, and by those of all shades of political opinion. I venture to think there is not one item in the programme which anyone can take exception to. There is the large scheme of Commercial Union, but short of that there are also practical questions of great import which all help on and lead up to the great cause which we are all so earnestly working for—(cheers).

The LORD MAYOR then put the resolution, which was carried unanimously.

Charles Tupper

SIR CHARLES TUPPER, Bart. :

I have been charged with the agreeable duty of moving the following resolution :—

> " That this meeting expresses its thanks to the Court of Common Council for granting the use of the Guild-hall, and to the Right Hon. the Lord Mayor for his kindness in presiding on this occasion "—(cheers).

I may say that I had the honour of forming a portion of the Conference, under the able presidency of Sir John Lubbock, who is on the platform, to arrange for the organi-sation of this League ; and when I say that the prime consideration—the great feature—in connection with this movement is for the purpose of maintaining and strengthen-ing the connection that exists between the United Kingdom and outlying portions of the Empire, I am sure I have stated that which will satisfy you all that this ancient hall was never appropriated to a more important and more useful purpose than it has served to-day, and that the Lord Mayor has never lent the countenance of his great office to any cause that is more worthy of acceptance of the people of this great Empire—(cheers). His Grace the Duke of Devonshire has called attention to the checks that have been encountered in the progress of this great question of Imperial unity. Another honourable gentle-man has referred to the fact that comparatively little progress has been made. But I confess that, looking to the conservative character of this great country, I am only surprised that so much progress has been made during the time this subject has specially engaged the attention of statesmen. It is true that some obstacles have been met with, that some of the more sanguine expectations of public men, not only in this great heart of the Empire, but also in the various Colonies, have been shown to be not entirely practicable, but I do not regard that as a check, but rather as a mark of progress, of what has been attained—that by close and careful examination on the part of public men, embracing both the great parties in this country and the self-governing Colonies, measures that were supposed to be practicable have been found not to be such as would attain the object this great organisation had in view. The Imperial Federation League, in my judgment, did most valuable work. That League, founded by that eminent statesman, the Right Hon. W. E. Forster—that League which has had ` the countenance of leaders of both parties in this country, and some of the most eminent men—that League, having for its object the unity of the Empire, has produced, has disseminated, has, in fact, indoctrinated the public mind of the people of this great country, and also in the outlying portions of the Empire, with the vital importance that it is not only to this country, but also to the Colonies themselves, that this connection should not only be maintained, but should also be strengthened, and, if possible, rendered more indissoluble than ever—(cheers). I believe the statement contained in the constitution of this League, that one of the most important measures that can be taken for the consolidation of this great Empire, embracing no less than some eleven million square miles of the globe, and no smaller population than 384 millions— I believe that no greater work can be undertaken than to consolidate and give additional strength to the security for the permanence of this, the mightiest Empire the world has ever seen—(cheers). Among those projects, that which is put in the forefront of this League is that trade is one of the most important and most significant means by which that can be attained. Sometimes even figures are eloquent, and eloquent statistics are contained in the trade returns of this country, for they show that in 1894 the exports of British and Irish produce to our self-governing Colonies and the British West Indies amounted to 51s. 8d. *per capita*, while the United States of

America took something less than 6s. per head, and France and Germany only 7s. 2d. per head. I think this is most eloquent in proving not only to the people of this country, but to the Colonies themselves, that there are no better means by which the trade of this great Empire—the trade of the United Kingdom—can be expanded and developed than by cultivating these great Colonial possessions which are to-day, I say, an object not only of admiration but of envy to other countries. I did not intend to go into the question of preferential trade, because although the platform on which the League is founded is broad enough for the advocates of preferential trade, it is not necessarily a part of its constitution that it should be carried out. The Duke of Devonshire has pointed out some of the difficulties that lay in the way, and has referred to the terms and limitations that have been indicated by the distinguished man who now occupies the position of Secretary of State to the Colonies. But while I do not go into the question, I may say that on a recent occasion, at the General Election in the Dominion of Canada, I urged the question of preferential trade—the adoption of a policy by which trade within the Empire would be maintained on different and more favourable grounds than that between any part of the Empire and foreign countries. While I made it an object of prime consideration and importance, and advocated it, as I believe it is one of the means by which the progress and prosperity of this great Empire can be immensely increased, I may say that the question is not a party question. The eminent French Canadian gentleman who is now Prime Minister of Canada, and who succeeded myself, declared in the face of the electorate that he was strongly in favour of preferential trade between the United Kingdom and Canada. I was not going to raise this question, but this platform is broad enough to enable the advocates of it to stand side by side with those who may entertain the opinion that it is an object not within our reach for a considerable period. I was glad to hear my friend Sir Westby Perceval, who speaks with authority as one of the most eminent men in the Australasian Colonies of which we are so proud—I was glad to hear him speak as he did on this question, and to regard it as one which at no very remote period would be looked upon with greater favour than it is at present. But while referring to my friend's remarks I may express the satisfaction with which I read in this morning's *Standard* the welcome intelligence that the Legislative Council of the important Colony of Victoria, in Australia, had not only passed a resolution, but passed it unanimously, in favour of a Conference being held at no distant date in London for the purpose of promoting the very object of this British Empire League—(cheers). This great meeting to-day at the Guildhall, presided over by the Lord Mayor, where we have had the opportunity of listening to the statesmanlike and admirable address of an eminent member of the British Government, receives, I am delighted to know, additional zest from the declaration of an important Australian Colony that the Legislature of that Colony, with entire unanimity, are prepared to act side by side with us on the very principles that are contained in the constitution of the League. I listened also with profound interest to the important statement made by the Duke of Devonshire with reference to the question of defence. I may say as far as that matter is concerned that there is no portion of this great Empire which, in my judgment, has not been engaged in steadily doing its utmost for the defence of the Empire. I say that every man who has gone into Canada to swell the British population there is a source of additional strength and security to this great Empire—I say that the enormous indebtedness which the self-governing Colonies have incurred has been expended largely in the development and opening up of those Colonies, and filling those countries that were weak and powerless with a British population prepared to defend themselves with their life's blood if necessary. Sometimes it has been said that the thread which binds the Colonies and the Mother Country together is a slender thread. I do not share that view—(cheers). I believe the feeling which pervades every portion of the British Empire and all its great outlying Colonies is that the British Constitution affords security for life and property that is not to be found in any other Constitution in the world. I believe the fact that every colonist knows that he enjoys this inestimable privilege under the ægis of the mightiest Empire in the world gives him a position of which he is justly proud, and which no consideration of any kind would induce him to surrender—(loud cheers). Strong as are sentimental ties, strong as is the personal devotion to the Queen, which pervades every portion of the Empire, strong as is the belief that the interests of the Colonies are conserved and will be preserved by maintaining those institutions of which we are now so proud, I still believe it is the duty of statesmen in this country, and in every part of the Empire, to address themselves to every means by which that tie can be strengthened—(cheers). I think I may be permitted on the present occasion, speaking on the question of defence, to say that although Canada has burdened herself with an enormous liability to construct a great inter-oceanic line of railway running from the Atlantic shores to the Pacific, although she has expended very large sums of money in organising and maintaining not only a small permanent military force but also a large body of 35,000 volunteer militiamen, although she has incurred other large liabilities in a manner calculated to secure in the best possible way the defence of this great Empire, yet on a recent occasion when a cloud arose, when there was a feeling of uneasiness in this country, and a feeling of uneasiness in Canada, as to our relations with the great Republic to the south of us, although every Canadian knows that no more dire misfortune could happen to him than any difficulty with that great Republic, not a public man, no portion of the Press in Canada but took their stand in defence of the position which the Government of England took on that occasion—

(cheers). They not only showed the entire unanimity of the Canadian people and their readiness to do and die in defence of the glorious institutions which they possess, but they gave us significant and practical evidence of the sincerity of that sentiment when they appropriated several million dollars for the purpose of providing the volunteer militia force of Canada with the best arms and accoutrements, and for further training that important force to act in defence of the Empire. I mention that by the way, in order to show that there is no part of Her Majesty's dominions more ready to recognise the responsibility that rests upon them than the people of Canada in regard to being prepared to contribute to the defence of this great Empire—(cheers). As his Grace made this subject an important portion of his speech, I may refer to the fact that the Lords of the Admiralty a few years ago, after most carefully considering the question as to how this great Empire could be best defended, came to the conclusion that there was no means by which a moderate amount of money could be expended so successfully for the purpose of strengthening that naval power which is regarded as the first line of defence in this country, as by the construction and the use of fast steamers intended for maintaining the closest and most rapid communication between the Mother Country and the outlying portions of the Empire—that there was no better means by which the strength of the British Navy could be added to by a moderate expenditure than by the Governments of the Colonies and the Government of this country combining their resources to have these great arteries of commerce, these great means of rapid mail and passenger communication, made and constructed under the direction of the Lords of the Admiralty, and put in a position at any moment to be available as Royal Naval Reserve cruisers. Reference is made in the constitution of this League to that important Conference to which the Duke of Devonshire alluded as having been held at Ottawa. That remark-

able assembly of the leading men of the Cape, of
South Africa, of Australasia, and of Canada—and
there was also present a representative, and an able
and distinguished representative, of the Imperial Government—after careful consideration resolved that one
of the most important measures that could be taken with
reference to the progress and prosperity of this Empire was
the establishment of a fast line of steamers between the
United Kingdom and Canada. Nature has given us the
geographical advantage that with steamers equal to those
running between this country and the city of New York, with
steamers of the same speed and capacity, letters and pas-
sengers could be laid down in the city of New York
quicker than by the most direct line from this country, and
that all the chief cities of Canada, all the western portion of
the United States of America, would not only be brought
much nearer to this country by that line of communication,
but that a great highway—a great Imperial highway—of
communication between this country, China, and Japan,
and Australasia would be established. I am glad to be
able, as I have taken a great interest in that important
measure, to tender my thanks to the present Secretary of
State for the Colonies and Her Majesty's Government for
the heartiness with which they entered not only into that
question as one of important Imperial concern, but
also into the question of the establishment of a cable on
British soil throughout, touching no foreign country, which
would give to the great Australian Colonies independent
communications, free from the dangers that exist at present.
I refer to the construction of the Pacific cable, which I
trust will at no distant date be brought to a conclusion.
I may mention in this connection that this League has
declared that one of the most important means of promoting
the unity of this great Empire is to adopt every means
not only of creating and expanding the trade between the
Mother Country and her Colonies, but also, by means of a
fast line of steamers, drawing the country closer together,

and by means of the Pacific cable continuing and securing the best interests of the great Colonies of Australasia, as well as of this country. Without further trespassing on your attention I will now propose this resolution, giving our hearty thanks for the use of this historic hall to the Court of Common Council, and to the Lord Mayor for presiding—(cheers).

SIR JOHN LUBBOCK, Bart., M.P.:

My Lord Mayor, your Grace, Ladies, and Gentlemen,— The Duke of Devonshire, in the admirable speech to which we listened in the early part of this afternoon, has very clearly stated the practical objects with which this League has been formed, and I believe there is not one of them more practical, or which will be more useful, than that of promoting a feeling of unity among all parts of the British Empire. The longer we live the more we see how much more men and women are influenced by their feelings than they are by reason. I suppose that most of us who are engaged in commerce will agree with me that if any South American Republic were to join the British Empire every one in that Republic would find themselves half again as rich the next morning—his land, houses, even his sheep and cattle, would be worth half again as much as they were the day before. Nevertheless, I do not suppose that the idea occurs to them. In the same way I believe that among the ties that bind together the British Empire, the recollection of our past history, our devotion to our Queen and country, is as strong as any of those material ties which knit us together. If, then, we admit that in one sense we have for a moment no definite changes to advocate, we still maintain that in promoting a patriotic sentiment, in holding up the British Flag, we are setting before ourselves a great and noble object. We have read with

John Lubbock

surprise many attacks on this country by foreign anonymous writers, but there is one great American economist, Mr. Wells, from whom I should like to quote a few generous words of appreciation. He says of our country :— " Wherever her Sovereignty has gone two blades of grass have grown where one grew before. Her flag, wherever it has been advanced, has benefited the country over which it floats, and has carried with it civilisation, the Christian religion, order, justice, and prosperity. England has always treated a conquered race with justice ; and what under her rule is the law for the white man is the law for his black, red, or yellow brother. And here we have one explanation for the fact that England alone of the nations has been successful in establishing and maintaining Colonies, and of the further extraordinary fact that a comparatively small insular country, containing less than forty million inhabitants, can successfully preside over the destinies of about 360,000,000 other members of the human race." We may all be proud of belonging to such an Empire ; it is with the object of strengthening, and, if possible, of knitting it together more closely that this British Empire League has been formed, and I think we shall all feel it to be appropriate that the first annual meeting should be held in this historic hall, and should be presided over by the Lord Mayor of the great metropolis of this Empire. I feel sure, therefore, that I shall be acting in accord with your wishes in seconding the resolution, to the effect that we should return our thanks to the Common Council for granting us the use of the Guildhall on this important occasion, and that we should offer our cordial thanks to the Lord Mayor for having graced the meeting by presiding over it—(cheers).

The resolution was then put to the meeting by Sir Charles Tupper, and was carried unanimously.

The LORD MAYOR : Your Grace, ladies and gentlemen, I am extremely obliged to you.

The proceedings then terminated.

D

SPEECHES DELIVERED IN THE HOUSE OF LORDS,

11th February, 1897.

___

The Earl of Minto asked the Lord President (the Duke of Devonshire) whether, in the existing scheme for utilising the naval and military forces of the Crown, the Volunteer force formed part of the plan for home defence ; and whether the recent increase of expenditure, whereby the Navy had been strengthened and augmented, rendered it in the opinion of her Majesty's Government less necessary to maintain the Volunteer force. He explained that the origin of the question was a statement made by the noble Duke in December last at a meeting of the British Empire League. Very great importance had been attached to that statement as denoting an entirely new departure in the matter of home defence and as affecting the question of the maintenance of the Volunteer force. The purport of the statement was understood in many quarters to be that the defence of the country was to be based on our sea supremacy, and that in future the country need have no fear of invasion on a large scale. Now if the idea of possible invasion was no longer to be entertained the *raison d'être* of the Volunteer force would disappear in the opinion of a large number of the rank and file, and the recruiting would consequently fall off. He hoped that the noble Duke would say that, in the opinion of the Government, the Volunteer force must continue to form a valuable part of the Army des ned for home defence.

The Duke of Devonshire : I am very much indebted to my noble friend for giving me the opportunity of saying a few words to correct some of the misapprehensions which have arisen in consequence of the speech which I made a short time ago at the meeting of the British Empire League, and at the same time of disavowing some of what appeared to be the most extraordinary conclusions which had been drawn from that speech. I was on that occasion speaking of the advantage which I thought might be derived from a repetition of such Colonial conferences as the conference which was held some time ago in this country. I was instancing as a subject which might be discussed at such a conference the conditions upon which the naval agreement with the Colonies of Australia, the term of which will shortly expire, might be renewed. I went on to speak of some of the principles which the home Government hopes that some of the Colonies are adopting, and will continue to adopt, in the way of preparations for their own defence. In the course of those observations I referred to a memorandum which has been for some years in existence, and which has been in the possession of all the Colonial Governments for some time. It is a memorandum which had hitherto been treated as a confidential document, and which is as regards some of its details still confidential in character, but I was permitted to refer to it as far as related to the general principles underlying Colonial defence. From that memorandum I quoted words some of which have been referred to by my noble friend. These were the words of the memorandum :—

" The maintenance of sea supremacy has been assumed as the basis of the system of Imperial defence against attack from over sea. This is the determining factor in shaping the defensive policy of the Empire, and is fully recognised by the Admiralty, who have accepted the responsibility of protecting all British territory abroad against organised invasion from the sea."

The memorandum went on to point out that complete freedom and independence of action was an essential condition of the efficiency of the Navy, but the presence of the fleet could not therefore be insured at all times at any particular point. The Colonies could not therefore be guaranteed against predatory attacks which might be made upon them by a force either of cruisers or of a small squadron of battleships. It went on further to point out the measures by which it was considered possible and desirable for the Colonies to place themselves in a position to secure themselves against attacks of that character. Now, I think the statement contained in that memorandum which I quoted may be open to comment, on the ground that perhaps it places too great a responsibility on the Navy, and that it attributes to the Admiralty

the assumption of a responsibility which it has perhaps hardly
to the fullest extent ever undertaken. But it is perfectly clear
in what sense that statement was addressed to the Colonial
Governments. The evident intention of that statement was
to limit the responsibility of the Imperial Government and to
point out clearly to the Colonies against what risks the home
Government could not undertake to protect them, and that it
was necessary, if they should be protected, they should undertake to protect themselves. This statement, as my noble
friend has said, has been treated in some quarters as the
announcement of an absolutely new policy of defence, and of
a policy of defence applicable not only to the Colonies, of
which I am speaking, but to the United Kingdom also. But
there is absolutely nothing new in the statement which I made
on that occasion, although I fully admit that some extremely
new deductions have been drawn from it—(hear, hear). In
the first place, the statement which I made applied only to the
Colonies and to Colonial defence. I did not conceive that any
sane Government ever imagined for a moment that the defence
of our possessions abroad against naval attack upon a large
scale could depend upon anything except the supremacy of our
Navy—(Cheers). No statesman, no soldier, and no sailor has
ever, I conceive, imagined that a serious attack by a great
maritime Power on one of our Colonial possessions could be
resisted by any fortifications, by the enlistment of any forces, or
by any maritime provisions within the power of the Colony
itself to make, and that their security against an attack of that
character could depend upon anything except the supremacy of
the Imperial Navy. But certain critics have fastened upon this
truism which, as I have explained, is borrowed from a memorandum long in existence of the Colonial Defence Committee,
and have exposed it to a most remarkable treatment. Some of
my critics have found fault with it because it referred only to
our possessions beyond the sea, and not to the United Kingdom
also ; while other critics have commented upon it as if it
referred to the defence of the United Kingdom as well as to
the Colonies ; and, having drawn the conclusion from it that,
our Navy is, as it ought to be, strong enough to resist organised
invasion either of our Colonial possessions or of our own
shores, have inferred that then any expenditure or any energy
applied to the erection of fortifications, of defensive works

or to the provision of adequate military establishments which are not of a mobile character, are so much expenditure and so much energy thrown away. I have no intention of entering at this time upon a discussion of the principles of Imperial defence. All I desire to do is to protest against the assumption that in that speech or at any other time I have advanced any new principles of defence either as concerns our Colonies or the United Kingdom. I was not authorised to make any announcement of any such new departure, and had not the slightest intention of doing it. The various additions which have been made to the Navy by the present and also by former Governments to increase the strength of the Navy and to insure our sea supremacy—these efforts all testify to the paramount importance which is attached not only by the present but by former Governments to the maintenance of our sea supremacy—(Opposition cheers) —which we look upon not only as our first line of defence but as our main security against attack—(Opposition cheers). I confess that, personally, I should have very little confidence in any defence organisation which was based on the probability of our permanently losing command of the sea, but between the permanent loss of the command of the sea and the possi- bility of a temporary reverse which might expose some portion of our coast to the risk of invasion there is a very wide interval, and, as far as I know, no Government has ever contemplated, and certainly this Government has never con- templated, the neglect of any precautions which might tend to the diminution of such risk. (Opposition cheers.) Another consideration which might appeal, I should have thought, even to those who rely most exclusively for our security upon the supremacy of our sea power, is that, as I have already pointed out, one of the most essential elements in the strength of our Navy is the freedom and independence of its action—(Oppo- sition cheers)—and the more you can guarantee the safety of vital points either abroad or at home without requiring the actual and immediate presence of the fleet the more you add to that freedom and independence of its action which consti- tutes one of the chief elements in its strength. Therefore, under these circumstances, I think that no Government either has been or can be indifferent to the necessity of making adequate provision either by means of fortifications, or defensive works, or by the provision of adequate military establish-ments in order to garrison them, and, if necessary, to take part in field operations in their support. No Government has ever neglected or can be indifferent to the necessity of such preparations. The question addressed to me by my noble friend refers only to the Volunteers. As regards the Volun-teers, I have no hesitation in assuring him that the Government consider that the Volunteer forces form an essential and indispensable part of our defensive arrangements. The measures' which were proposed to Parliament by my noble friend last year for strengthening the financial position of the Volunteers testify to the interest and appreciation of the services of that force by the Government, and I am informed that in the present year there will be a considerable addition asked for to the Volunteer Vote, caused by the increased number of efficients—an increase which I believe is partly due to the assistance which was given to them last year. The Volunteers who are represented on this occasion by my noble friend need be under no apprehension whatever that the impor-tance of maintaining both their numbers and their efficiency is in any way neglected or discouraged by the Government. I trust that after the explanation which I have been able to give the Volunteers will agree with me that any apprehensions which have been felt that their services are not held at their proper value by the Government are due not to anything which I have said on the part of her Majesty's Government, but to the totally unauthorised construction which has been placed on certain statements which I have made and for which, in my humble opinion, there was absolutely no warrant or foundation. I hope this answer may be satisfactory both to my noble friend and to the Volunteers.

The Earl of Kimberley : I have heard with very great satisfaction and no surprise the explanation given by the noble Duke, because I was for a long time connected with the Colonial Department and had opportunity of seeing documents at that time with reference to Colonial defence, and I very well indeed remember the document to which the noble Duke referred in his former speech. It is no new principle which is laid down in that document. It has invariably been the opinion of Governments of this country, with reference to Colonial defence, that the Navy, if it is to do its duty—which it cannot do unless it is free—must be supported by the Colonies in such a manner as to make predatory attacks upon them capable of resistance without the presence of the fleet. That has been a constantly observed condition. With regard to home defence, I have read with great interest and extreme surprise various effusions implying that the trust which this country must always mainly put in its Navy for the protection of our coasts exempts us from the necessity of making any other preparations. I am in no way qualified to speak upon questions either of naval or military tactics, but I should have supposed that if our fleet is to be perfectly free to engage the enemy at a distance from our shores, it might possibly happen that at some given moment it might not be available at some particular point. Suppose we suffered some minor reverse to some squadron which was not so powerful as our main fleet, might it not easily happen that an enemy might make a serious attack upon one of our dockyards? The protection of our dockyards against any such sudden attack seems to be a matter of extreme consequence to the interests of the nation. I merely instance that because no person would conceive it was a safe thing to leave our dockyards unprotected against any sudden attack. Instances might be multiplied ; and it seems to me that some preparations as regards fortifications— though I should not say very extensive fortifications—are very desirable, and that some preparations for fortifying important points, places where ships are built and where coal stores are accumulated for the use of the fleet, are absolutely indispensable. The meaning of that is not that you rely upon those fortifications or even the military preparations to meet an invasion, but that they are necessary supports for your first line of defence and indispensable to the free action of the fleet. Speaking with some knowledge of the views of previous Governments, I can most entirely confirm every word which has been so clearly and thoroughly stated by the noble Duke.

PRESS OPINIONS.

THE " TIMES," *December 4th*, 1896.

The objects of the British Empire League could not be more ably and lucidly set forth than in the most interesting speech delivered yesterday at the Guildhall by the Duke of Devonshire. That body is the successor of the defunct Imperial Federation League, which failed, as the Duke admitted with characteristic candour, because it attempted too much, and advocated ideas for which the time was not, and is not yet, ripe. Many of our readers will, no doubt, remember the difficulty felt by those who sympathised with the general aims of that league in finding any concrete expression for their aspirations which did not manifestly fail to adapt itself to the actual conditions of the Empire. They will also remember the ridicule which was poured not only upon the movement but upon the ideas that underlay it. Ideas, however, when they are sound, are nearly indestructible, and have a way of disengaging themselves from unsuitable environments which is found· extremely perplexing by superficial critics. Imperial Federation was not possible, at least at the time, and a league bearing its name and pledged to promote it was consequently doomed to failure. But Imperial Federation as conceived by the league was only one embodiment among many possible ones of the Imperial idea. It was not then attainable, it is not attainable even now, yet the unity of the Empire has been powerfully promoted by the efforts made to realise the impossible, and the Imperial Federation League is outlived by its works. The British Empire League pursues the same objects, but it takes lower ground, announces less far-reaching aspirations, and confines itself more strictly to the immediately practicable. The Duke of Devonshire stated the case with perfect accuracy when he said, " I believe that the idea of " Imperial unity as a sentiment, as an inspiration perhaps as it " has often been described, as a dream, is one which has " made progress and continues to make progress in the minds and convictions of men both at home and in the Colonies." That is much, perhaps as much as we have any right to expect, or as true wisdom would desire. Great movements are slow, and rapid evolution always provokes the apprehension of reaction. It may require some exceptional circumstances yet in the womb of time to crystallise the ideas which the British Empire League exists to foster. It is not given to man to create his opportunity, but it is within his power to be prepared to seize the opportunity when it offers. It is the function of the British Empire League, not a mean or unimportant one, to educate the minds of men at home and in our Colonies, in such wise that the crises which come unexpectedly to every State may find all disposed to seek safety in closer union.

Though the great Conference of 1887 did not produce all the tangible results that sanguine persons expected, it not only had a great moral effect, both within the Empire and upon the world at large, but it brought about the naval agreement whereby our Colonies actively associated themselves with the Mother Country in the work of defence. That agreement was for a limited term of years now approaching its close, and the Duke of Devonshire, speaking for the Government, declares that they attach the highest importance to its renewal. The precise terms are, of course, subject to reconsideration—that is implied in the fact of renewal being necessary. But in some form or other it is of great importance for the Empire at large that our Colonies should undertake some part of the general work of Imperial defence. It is not so much the pecuniary interests involved, or the addition to our naval strength, that gives importance to the naval agreement. What is chiefly valuable is its embodiment of the idea of Imperial unity, and the partial federation of the Empire which a combination for mutual defence implies. One permanent gain from the agreement is the careful study to which it led of the position of every Colony in a general scheme of defence. The Colonial Defence Committee has gone carefully into the question from the point of view of each particular Colony, has defined the duties which the Admiralty ought to undertake, the kind and degree of local defence which the Colonies ought to provide, and the attacks to which they may be subject short of great movements against which the Navy will take precautions. The details are necessarily confidential as between the Mother Country and each Colony concerned, but the general principles on which the scheme is based are not only public property, but in the view of the Government cannot be too widely made known.

THE "MORNING POST," *December 4th*, 1896.

The Duke of Devonshire shares with the late Lord Derby a reputation for coolheadedness and caution which have always commanded the respect of Englishmen, while the more showy qualities of others have excited their admiration and enthusiasm. No idea can be regarded as wholly fantastic or illusory which has once secured the patronage and adherence of the slow-moving and practical Statesman who is now the Lord President of the Council. The mere fact that the Duke of Devonshire is the President of the British Empire League frees that organisation from the risk of the reproach that its objects are chimerical or quixotic. His presence at the meeting held yesterday at the Guildhall, under the auspices of that League, and with the Lord Mayor in the chair, was a guarantee that the aims which the League seeks to accomplish are feasible and desirable. The speech in which the Duke of Devonshire recommended to the favourable attention of the merchants and commercial magnates of the chief City of the Empire the importance and necessity of consolidating the resources and federating the strength of the Mother Country and her Colonies ought to do much towards popularising an idea that has made great advances in a practical direction in recent years. It ought further to give effective aid to the efforts of those who are striving to bring within the area of practical statesmanship that which until lately was regarded as the Utopian dream of extravagant patriots. It was not merely as a distinguished member of Lord Salisbury's Cabinet or as President of the British Empire League that the presence of the Duke of Devonshire at yesterday's gathering was as welcome as it was significant. No one who heard him insisting upon the urgent need of a practical measure of Federation, which with the growth of our Colonies might make available for Imperial defence the whole resources of the British Empire and her Colonies, can have forgotten that he is the President of the Committee of National Defence founded by Lord Salisbury, which includes not only the Secretary of State for War and the First Lord of the Admiralty, but the Chancellor of the Exchequer and the Commander-in-Chief. The resolution which was moved by the Duke was somewhat vague in its character, and it sought to pledge the meeting to a programme the items of which have not been generally or widely explained. It is sufficient, however, to examine the recommendations of the Duke himself in order to ascertain the objects he, as President of the League, is anxious to promote. A great advance has been made, or rather a complete revolution has been effected, in the relations that existed between the United Kingdom and the Colonies since the late Lord Granville, Lord Kimberley, and Lord Ripon were the controlling spirits at the Colonial Office. It is not so many years ago since the attitude of the Secretary of State towards the Colonies had rendered Separation, and not Federation, a matter of almost immediate certainty. To-day, owing to the loyal spirit evinced by the Colonies on more than one occasion of the Mother Country's difficulties, and to the sympathetic acknowledgment of the loyal offer of their services made by the responsible Ministers of the Crown, the idea of Separation would not be tolerated and the idea of Federation is eagerly fostered, though the scheme by which it is to be effected has not yet been devised. Our Colonial Empire was not acquired in a day, and its consolidation is not to be accomplished in a year or in a decade. Experience, as the Duke of Devonshire wisely remarked, has taught those who have this cause in hand the necessity of caution, of moderation, of patience, and perhaps even of humility.

The Imperial Federation League, with which the names of the late Mr. Forster, of Lord Rosebery, and the late Mr. Stanhope were so closely and honourably connected, has, it is true, been voluntarily dissolved. The spirit, however, that actuated those who galvanised into a living actuality the sentiment of binding in indissoluble bonds the Mother Country and the Colonies did not expire with the dissolution of the League. The work of those who passed away all too soon for their country's good was not without effect. From the ashes of the Imperial Federation League the British Empire League has, phoenix-like, arisen with fresh vigour, and if its aims are not so ambitious and its methods not so precipitate as those of its predecessor its object is to carry to completion the noble work which Mr. Forster set on foot and Mr. Stanhope strove to forward. The Duke of Devonshire reminded his audience that both Lord Salisbury and Mr. Chamberlain were keenly in sympathy with the objects of the late League, and he did its founders no more than justice when he acknowledged that they had called the attention of the subjects of the Queen both at home and in the Colonies to a question of the most serious magnitude, and one affecting the future and the unity of the British Empire. That the efforts of the late League were not wholly barren was proved by the assembling of the Conference in London in 1887. It was attended by eminent representatives from all our Colonies, and an English statesman presided over its deliberations. A scheme of Federation was propounded which proved to be too ambitious and comprehensive. Men's minds were not ripe for the practical development of a plan the idea of which was only in its infancy. Thus far the Conference was a failure, but it bore useful fruit in other respects. Interest has again revived in the possibility of forming a union on a commercial basis between Great Britain and her Colonies, which may be the forerunner of an ultimate closer union for the purposes of the Military and Naval defence of every part of the Empire by every one of its constituent members. The Duke of Devonshire was careful to defend Mr. Chamberlain from a reproach that has been recently levelled against him by leading members of the Opposition. He has been taunted with having put forward proposals for an Imperial Zollverein which have been ignored and rejected by the Colonies. It has been pointed out in these columns, and was urged by the Duke yesterday, that Mr. Chamberlain put forward no scheme. He suggested that if the Colonies could agree amongst themselves upon a common fiscal policy, to which they were prepared to invite the adherence of the Mother Country with a view to fighting the hostile tariffs imposed by foreign Powers, they would be met with cordiality at Downing Street instead of with an insolent rebuff as in former days. The practical beginning of Federation must commence with the Colonies themselves. Australasia must form a Confederation similar to that which has been established in North America, and South Africa must follow suit. When these dependencies of the

Crown are agreed upon a common line of action amongst themselves the time will have arrived for endeavouring to establish an Imperial Federation, which, if constructed on a solid basis, might bid defiance to all the world besides. . . . . . Both at home and in the Colonies the claim put forward by the Duke for the co-operation of the Colonies will, we feel sure, be recognised as a fair and legitimate one. The spirit of loyal devotion already displayed by the Colonies induces us to share the hope expressed by the Duke of Devonshire that, stimulated by the example that has been set to them, they will not hesitate to do all that is necessary to discharge the very moderate share of the duty which is to be imposed upon them.

THE "STANDARD," *December 4th*, 1896

The Duke of Devonshire yesterday made a notable addition to the list of important political deliverances of which the City of London has been the appropriate scene. As president of the British Empire League, he moved the principal resolution at the meeting held at the Guildhall to celebrate the entry of that body upon the stage of organised activity. Excellent as the speech was throughout, the portion in which the Duke set forth, with the utmost clearness and deliberation, the principles upon which the Ministerial scheme of Imperial Defence is based, must claim special attention. To trace the efforts hitherto made to bring about a comprehensive Federation of the Empire, to examine the more limited suggestions recently put forward by Mr. Chamberlain for the study of a plan of fiscal or commercial union, fell naturally within the scope of the Duke's review. But he was obliged to confess that, as yet, little or no advance had been made towards the realisation of either ideal. With the agreement for safeguarding our outlying States and Dependencies from hostile attack, the case happily stands otherwise. Not only was a plan framed, but it has stood the test of practical trial. The Conference of eminent Colonial Statesmen, which was held here in 1887, was more than an eloquent symbol of the unity of the Empire. It bequeathed to everyday statesmanship the conception of joint arrangements between the several Colonies and the Mother Country for protecting the more exposed positions. As an outcome of the

Conference, the covenants for naval co-operation were entered into with the Australian Colonies and New Zealand. It is true that a rough-and ready criterion was adopted for the apportionment of the expense. For the additions which, in pursuance of this understanding, the Mother Country made to its Fleets, with a view to strengthening our Naval armaments in Colonial waters, the Colonies paid the interest on the cost of construction and a percentage of the charge for maintenance. So far, a vital principle was established and justified in practice ; but now the term for which the agreement was made is about to expire, and the question arises whether it is to lapse. Every consideration which, in the first instance, recommended the joint system forbids its abandonment ; and we cannot doubt that the Governments of Australasia will welcome the Duke of Devonshire's emphatic assurance that the British Cabinet "attach the greatest importance to its renewal in one form or another." . . . . To put the idea in the briefest compass, the Mother Country is ready to guarantee the outlying States from anything like organised invasion, by asserting an incontestable mastery of the sea. More than this, or perhaps we should rather say incident to this, is the obligation uncompromisingly accepted by Great Britain, of fortifying and holding all ports and positions essential to Naval supremacy. Thus all the Imperial resources will be devoted to the due equipment of coaling stations, dockyards, and so forth, on which the Fleets will depend. . The positions chosen for these purposes have all been selected : nothing is left to uncertainty or chance. But, in carrying out the pledge of absolute protection from organised attack, the Imperial Government claim a thoroughly free discretion as to the disposal of their forces. They may, for instance, decide that a certain Colony may best be saved by action on the high seas, and may not think it expedient to detail a single vessel for local services. It is here that the duty of the Colonial communities begins No Navy, however powerful, no strategic foresight, however keen, can ensure every point of the accessible coastline from the possibility of a raid. But so long as our ships command the ocean there is no possibility of a descent, and it is not unreasonable to ask our fellow subjects, whether in the Canadian Dominion or in Polynesia, to maintain such local military forces, such forts, and such warships as will deter an enemy from making any annoying demonstration, or, should the attempt be made, will promptly baffle invasion. The Mother Country, in a word, will keep up the barrier against Armadas, and will trust to the Colonies to give a good account of chance cruisers or casual raids. Nothing facilitates the settlement of a problem so much as a distinct perception of the various duties which have to be discharged by the contracting parties, and there is every reason to hope that Colonial Statesmanship will cordially accept the division of functions indicated by the Duke of Devonshire as the basis for the revised covenants, which are to replace the expiring understanding.

We may, therefore, look forward with satisfaction to the early assembling of another Conference, in which, possibly, delegates from Australasia will meet delegates from Canada. It is in dealing with needs as they arise that the sentiment of Imperial unity can best be developed, and no one who pays any regard to the tokens of storm in the International firmament can hesitate to recognise as a paramount and urgent obligation the perfecting of the framework of Imperial defence. But there is no reason why these gatherings of British Statesmen from beyond the seas should not, when the primary task is finished consider the possibilities of a larger and closer union. We must not conclude, from the frankness with which the Duke of Devonshire referred to the comparative absence of practical results, that the various strivings towards Federation have been barren failures. There are impediments, the seriousness of which no patriot will seek to disguise. Each of the outlying States of the Empire has grown up in its own way, and the variety of circumstances under which they have shaped their several courses continues to operate. Communities which have from infancy to manhood been accustomed to one fiscal method cannot immediately escape from the economic consequences of their peculiar system. But it is much to have set up firmly the ideal of ultimate co-ordination or assimilation even though, for the time being, surrounding conditions are too rigid to permit of any approach to union in fact. It is true that the original Imperial Federation League has been dissolved ; but if it had not existed the policy of agreement for naval defence would still be a dream. Working from a narrower and, therefore, firmer base, its successor the British Empire League will gradually get nearer to the desired goal. Nor ought disappointment to be expressed at the absence of any encouraging response from the Colonies to the suggestions thrown out by Mr. Chamberlain as to the feasibility of closer relations in the matter of commercial exchange. Provided the splendid series of States which, scattered all over the world, owe allegiance to the Empress-Queen, keep constantly in view the excellence of union as an end, there must be a tendency in domestic developments to make Federation less difficult.

THE "DAILY NEWS," *December 4th,* 1896.

FEDERATION IN IMPERIAL DEFENCE.—The greatest of all questions which have to be answered by the present generation of Englishmen is the question of Imperial unity. Is the British Empire to become a series of independent States, or to make a reality of that unity which at the present time rests more on sentiment than on practical organisation? If the unity of the Empire is to be attained, in what way is it to be embodied either in political institutions or in military and naval organisation? The speech which the Duke of Devonshire delivered at the Guildhall was of the utmost interest and importance as bearing upon these momentous questions. The cause of Imperial Federation, so far as it has been advocated in the practical and not merely in the sentimental sphere, has passed through three phases. At first its advocates approached the problem on the political side. We firmly believe that the political genius of the British race will in time be equal to the solution even of that problem, which is at once the most important and the most difficult that has ever been proposed. But at present it cannot be said that on the political side the idea of Imperial Federation has embodied itself in any practical shape whatever. It remains as the Duke of Devonshire said yesterday, "a dream," or, as we should prefer to phrase it, an ideal. The second attempt to promote the cause of Imperial Federation was made on the commercial side; but here also no practical advance has been secured. Mr. Chamberlain has admitted that the scheme of the Ottawa Conference was hopeless, and the alternative proposals which he himself threw out have met with no favour. The third and most hopeful stage of the movement is the military and naval stage, and it was to this that the Duke of Devonshire addressed himself yesterday. In this sphere, and in this sphere alone, the

Colonial Conference of 1887 bore practical fruit, though its moral significance as a visible symbol of the unity of the Empire was in all directions fruitful of good. The practical fruit was the naval agreement which was made between the Mother Country and the Australian Colonies and the Colony of New Zealand, and the terms of which we summarise in another column. This agreement lapses in 1898, and the declarations of the Duke of Devonshire were made with a view to the discussions which will shortly ensue upon its proposed renewal. Those declarations were of the utmost importance as a statement of Imperial policy. Not many years ago the author of " Problems of Greater Britain" recorded as a remarkable instance of past Imperial carelessness that the very principles upon which the burden of defence should be divided between ourselves and the Colonies, and the proportions in which it should be borne, had never been settled. This reproach is no longer justified, for the scheme which the Duke of Devonshire was authorised by his colleagues to expound yesterday is clear and precise. . . . . . . The existing agreement with the Australian Colonies and New Zealand expires in 1898, and the Duke of Devonshire indicates that before that time another Colonial Conference will be called to consider the question of renewing that agreement, and of forming similar arrangements, perhaps with other Colonies. The Britsh Empire League, which has been formed to take the place of the defunct Imperial Federation League, and which the Duke of Devonshire inaugurated yesterday, will do much to justify its existence if it helps to form public opinion in the direction indicated. The Colonies are and aspire to be great commercial communities, and some of their citizens talk as if that end were in itself all-sufficient and self-secure. They would do well to remember the saying of Tocqueville, " Reason shows and experience proves that no " commercial prosperity can be durable if it cannot be united, " in case of need, to naval force." As integral parts of the British Empire, the Colonies enjoy the best security known in the modern world—the security of the British Navy. The people of the Mother Country have of late years taken upon themselves heavy and ever-increasing financial burdens in order to make that security yet more sure. If the present or any succeeding Government should in the discharge of its solemn

E

responsibility declare that yet further sacrifices are necessary to retain for the British Empire the supremacy of the sea, those sacrifices also will, we believe, be cheerfully borne. It ought not under these circumstances be too much to hope that the Colonies will on their part do all that is necessary to discharge the very moderate share which the Duke of Devonshire's scheme imposes upon them in the common work of Imperial defence. If the British Empire League can firmly establish the principle of the unity of the Empire and its defences, it will succeed in securing alike to the whole and to every part, the greatest attainable protection, and it will help to solve the greatest and most momentous question of our generation in the way most conducive to the peace and civilisation of the world.

THE " PALL MALL GAZETTE," *December 4th*, 1896.

STEADY DOES IT.— . . . .The Imperial Federation League, in fact, got hold of the wrong end of the stick ; it went slap-dash at the political unity of the Empire. The time is, we should not care to calculate how much, too unripe for that ; political unity will come, but a good many other things will have to be screwed down into their places first. The place of yesterday's meeting, the City, was significant. The English race is best approached through its pockets ; we are a nation of—but that has been said before. But even here steady does it. The Ottawa scheme never moved half an inch, and the response to the shadowy commercial reciprocity throwings-out, which Mr. Chamberlain purposely and wisely left very vague, has not been too encouraging. Suggestions from business men are what the Duke invites, and that is really all that can be done at present. But there is Lord Lansdowne's "insurance"; when all is said, something may be done at once there. Colonel Hutton told us the other day something of what Australia was doing ; the Duke of Devonshire has now made a most important pronouncement as to what is being done here. His statement as to the Colonial Defence Committee's arrangements was valuable for itself, and valuable because he was "not only permitted, but asked " to make it, which shows that the right people are awake. The agreement with the Australian Colonies expires in 1898, and it must be renewed and strengthened. So far the situation stands thus. The Imperial Government guarantees (1) that we shall hold the sea and make it impossible to invade any colony in force. Very good ; Mr. Goschen must be kept with his toe right up to the line, that is all. (2) It will secure all coaling, refitting, and repairing stations. Quite as good. But (3) the Colonies themselves are required to undertake the defence of their commercial ports, to put themselves into a position capable of withstanding any attack by one or two isolated cruisers. The Imperial authorities reserve full power to move their ships to any point necessitated by the general situation ; there must be no locking up of ships in front of a settlement. We have every trust that the Colonies may be relied upon to play up to this ; and, that being so, we are sure that the best first step to unite a race which has the sea in its blood is being taken.

THE " ST. JAMES'S GAZETTE," *December 4th*, 1896.

SACRIFICES ON BOTH SIDES.—We asked the other day what the Imperial Defence Committee was doing. The Duke of Devonshire's interesting and important statement at the Guildhall yesterday is the answer. Everybody will learn with pleasure that a reasoned and coherent scheme of Imperial strategy has been worked out. The details are confidential ; the general plan is not, and the Duke of Devonshire was able to give it. As far as one can judge by the brief outline he sketched, it goes generally on the right lines. The fundamental principle is that all parts of the Empire must bear a share in the burdens of military and naval efficiency. The Colonies are prepared to pay a fair proportion of the expense instead of leaving it all to be borne by the Mother Country. There is, it must be admitted, something humiliating to the pride of prosperous high-spirited little nations, in the notion that toiling taxpayers in English counties and Scotch boroughs must pay the whole costs of defending their ports from raiding cruisers and their coasters from prowling privateers. Since 1887 the Australians have contributed something towards the Imperial Navy by paying their share of the maintenance of a smart little local squadron. It is something, and we hope it is to be followed by similar arrangements in regard to the Cape and Canada. . . . . It is a bold and sensible project, and we rejoice to hear that the Colonial Governments have shown no reluctance to incur the sacrifices necessary to carry it out. Imperial Defence is a popular cause ; but, like other great things, it cannot be compassed without self-sacrifice. The Colonies will have to spend money and time, in order to get their local militias to the requisite state of efficiency, and to supply them with staff, artillery, war material, and transport necessary to enable them to take the field at short notice, for a little campaign, against the troops of a great military Power. For the people of these islands there are some further sacrifices to be made too. If anybody supposes that the provision of small Colonial defence corps, and a great Imperial Navy, will enable us to leave the Army comfortably alone, he is likely to be enlightened in the course of next Session. If the Colonists are prepared to incur, what to them at least must be serious military obligations, they will ask us to take ours in a similar spirit. Apparently we are not inclined to accept even the modified form of compulsory military service which is the law in most of the Colonies. But our two complete army corps—say 60,000 men—properly equipped and capable of foreign service we ought to have ; and these we have assuredly not got at present.

THE "WESTMINSTER GAZETTE," *December 4th*, 1896.

The British Empire League—the successor in a direct line of the old Imperial Federation League—held a very successful meeting in the City yesterday, at which the Duke of Devonshire made an important speech. Next year the ten years' arrangement with the Australasian Colonies, by which they contribute towards the cost of the Navy, will expire, and as it is proposed to ask them for rather more money in the future, the Duke, in a thoroughly business-like way, took the opportunity of explaining the principles upon which the Colonial Defence Committee has settled the defence of the Empire. Briefly, the Mother Country undertakes the entire responsibility for maintaining our sea supremacy, provided (1) she has entire control of the Navy, and (2) the Colonies undertake the task of local defence. The Duke of Devonshire yesterday attempted to "regularise" our relation with the Colonies, and certainly cordial co-operation in Imperial defence must be a strong factor in building up true Imperial unity.

DEFENCE OF THE EMPIRE.—The speech of the Duke of Devonshire yesterday before the British Empire League contained a most important pronouncement on the subject of Imperial policy. We refer to his declaration that the Colonies are to be invited to bear their part in the new scheme of Imperial Defence. The invitation is certain to be cordially accepted by the Colonies, for under the scheme they will receive much more than an equivalent for the small sacrifices they will be called upon to make. The Navy will still guarantee their security against a general attack ; but the Colonists are asked to undertake, by the use of their own local resources, to deal effectively with sporadic raids. Whilst the proposals adumbrated by the Duke of Devonshire do not involve the imposition of any heavy burden, they must infallibly deepen the sense of fraternity and inter-dependence as between the Colonists and the Mother Country. Of course, the principles underlying the scheme are not entirely novel. They have already been recognised in the case of our Australasian Colonies. By the Naval agreement now in existence, the Australian Colonies and New Zealand undertook to pay the interest on the cost of construction, and a part of the cost of maintenance, of a considerable addition to the fleet, to be maintained in Australasian waters for the protection of British and Colonial commerce. This agreement, as the Duke of Devonshire observed, was the first recognition which had ever been made by any of the Colonies of their duty to contribute to the support of the Imperial Navy. Very soon the term of that agreement will expire ; but there is every reason to believe that it will be renewed. Practically speaking, the scheme outlined by the Duke of Devonshire is an all-round application of the principles underlying that agreement to British possessions in every part of the world. . . . .
No one here or in the Colonies can complain of these principles as being unfair or unjust. The Duke of Devonshire spoke of the vast obligations incurred by the British people in order to strengthen the Fleet and enable it to fulfil its responsibilities, not only to the Mother Country but also to the Colonies. He added an expression of hope that the Colonies, stimulated by this example and by that of the Australians, will

do all that is necessary to discharge the "very moderate share" of duties which it is proposed to impose upon them. This appeal to the local patriotism of the Colonies, and this invitation to co-operate in a scheme of defence for the whole Empire of which they form a part are certain to evoke a hearty response.

THE "MANCHESTER GUARDIAN," *December 4th*, 1896.

The Duke of Devonshire made a speech of great importance and of a highly satisfactory character at the meeting held yesterday in the City of London by the British Empire League. . . . . . . To politicians proper, the most interesting point about them is this—that the Colonies are evidently to be asked to bear a larger share of the charges for Imperial Defence than they have hitherto borne. In equity they ought to do so, inasmuch as they would in the case of a serious war be dependent to a great extent for their safety upon ships hitherto maintained almost wholly by the home taxpayers. But we have still to see how far the self-governing Colonies will consent to increase their contributions without obtaining a share of the control of expenditure and of the Imperial policy of which the jointly owned Navy would in the last resort be the instrument.

THE "LEEDS MERCURY," *December 4th*, 1896.

When our leading statesmen begin to betray an uneasy feeling because they have not made a tour of the Empire of whose affairs they are responsible directors, it is evident, as Lord Rosebery remarked, that the days of a Little England party are at an end. Though the Imperial Federation League was unfortunately dissolved after years of invaluable propagandist work, yet the course of events conspired to promote its objects and served to reveal in the most signal and significant manner the depth and reality of the attachment existing between the Colonies and the Mother Country. Whilst it cannot be said that much progress has been made towards a closer union between the various parts of the Empire, yet it is no longer possible to question that the desire for practical steps in that direction is very widely entertained both in this country and the Colonies. . . . . It cannot be doubted that our Australian Colonies will feel the necessity of taking upon themselves afresh this comparatively small share of the cost of their defence. But it is certainly desirable that the whole question of Colonial Defence and the part which the Colonies shall take in the matter shall be fully discussed at another Conference convened for the purpose.

THE "GLASGOW HERALD," *December 4th*, 1896.

One thing must be made abundantly clear in all these discussions, and that is, that Great Britain will take no steps which involve any risk to her adopted commercial policy. Inter-Imperial Free Trade may involve no such risk, but the Colonies are hardly ripe for the discussion of such plan, and until they are another Inter-Colonial Conference will not do much good. What the British Empire League, as we understand from the Duke of Devonshire, is to do in present circumstances is to collect such materials and such a body of commercial opinion as may form the basis of discussion when the time comes for the holding of another Conference.

THE "ABERDEEN FREE PRESS," *December 4th*, 1896.

The principle of common and joint action by the Mother Country and the Colonies for the common purpose of Imperial Defence has already been affirmed in the public policy of the Empire. It receives a little development in the scheme which the Duke of Devonshire unfolded in London yesterday, but not an extension that is in the least likely to excite opposition by going in advance of the ideas and sentiments of the Colonists in matters that so intimately concern them.

THE "NOTTINGHAM GUARDIAN," *December 5th*, 1896.

The speech delivered the other night by the Duke of Devonshire upon the subject of Imperial Defence will have caused widespread satisfaction. It was one of the most important political speeches delivered for a long period, and both the tone and the matter of it were excellent. . . . . It will be seen, therefore, how important the scheme is which the Imperial Defence Committee is working out. There is no doubt that it will be cordially accepted in the Colonies. The people who live there belong to the same race as ourselves. They have inherited the same martial and Imperial traditions, and they are proud of their connection with the Empire. That they would fight in defence of their independence and of their material interests, to say nothing of the reputation of the race from which they have sprung, is certain, and while we all of us hope that the necessity for fighting will never arise, we cannot ignore the necessity of providing against a danger which, to say the least, will always be imminent. This is the first time, we believe, in modern British history, that the necessity for adequate defensive preparation has been fully realised, but it is certain that if, in the past, there had always been as keen and general a recognition of the necessity of defensive preparations as now prevails, the British Empire would have escaped many disasters, and have been both stronger and richer than it is to-day. ——

THE "NOTTINGHAM EXPRESS," *December 5th*, 1896.

It is practically the outcome of the defunct Imperial Federation League, from whose ashes, Phœnix-like, it arises ; but it is essentially more practical in its programme, and for that reason may be expected to enjoy a longer lease of life and a career of greater usefulness. The Federation League expressed a noble, if somewhat nebulous, ideal ; but failed in defining the means whereby it sought to attain its end. An organisation which can only point to something it would attain, but cannot say definitely and decisively " Here is the way," can scarcely hope to accomplish anything practicable. Such was the case with the defunct League ; but, this notwithstanding, it did much good during its existence by fostering the Imperial idea, and if it did nothing to make Imperial Federation more real it certainly did nothing to tarnish the ideal ; we even believe it did not a little to bring public opinion nearer to the ideal than it had been before the League came into existence. . . . . It seems to us to be almost entirely satisfactory, largely based as it is on the sound principle of mutual co-operation. It means that while the Imperial Government is ready to undertake the fullest responsibility for the defence of the Empire, it calls upon Colonial authorities to bear their part as well, and we imagine the scheme will commend itself as much to our kith and kin beyond the seas as to their friends at home.

THE "BELFAST EVENING TELEGRAPH," *December 4th*, 1896.

At present the aim of the British Empire League is not to frame constitutions or to elaborate commercial systems, but to furnish a channel of communication between Englishmen at home and abroad, to discuss difficulties, and, if possible, to remove misunderstandings which still stand in way of a more complete Imperial unity. This object, if not ambitious, is important, and it will be greatly furthered by the wise guidance of the Lord President of the Council.

——

THE "SYDNEY MORNING HERALD," *December 8th*, 1896.

A difficulty in the way of renewing the agreement might easily arise if the Colonies were to be asked to modify the existing agreement to the extent of leaving themselves open to be deprived of the ships for which they pay so much annually, at the moment when they would·seem to most need their protection, and independently of their consent.

The practical question for the consideration of the Imperial authorities is whether or not it is worth while to raise such a difficulty, when the sentiment of race as well as that of self-interest would secure the same result without the Colonies being asked to alter a line in the existing agreement. If some of the Colonies feel themselves aggrieved now because they see less of the ships of the Squadron than other Colonies do, or because the Colony which pays the largest contribution towards the maintenance of the Fleet and which has been at some expense to provide a residence for the Admiral and sites for Admiralty stores is more favoured in this respect than they, a suggestion like this will only add to their complaints. The grievance may be baseless, or it may even be ill-advised from the standpoint of naval experts, who must be supposed to be the best judges of the effectiveness of naval tactics, and the best means of securing it. But it must be remembered that it is not the Colonies that are dissatisfied, but those who raise the question of a change in the existing agreement. If the British Empire League thinks of Imperial defence first, there is nothing abnormal in the fact that the Colonies have a tendency to look nearer home and think of Australasian defence, since it is on the basis of that understanding that the Auxiliary Squadron came into existence. The Colonies have now no desire to part with their ships, and they do not seriously begrudge the contributions towards their maintenance. Nor does any practical objection really exist to their being employed in conjunction with the China or the Pacific Fleet should occasion require. But there is a sentimental preference for the feeling that the ships belong to our own system of coast defence, and it is one not undeserving of consideration.

THE "SYDNEY TELEGRAPH," *December 8th.* 1896.

We have to consider what our position would be while the matter was in dispute. The use of a local fleet is to protect these shores against the ravages they would be exposed to during the progress of a war. That was certainly what was in the mind of the Colonies when the present agreement regarding the Auxiliary Squadron was made, but the idea now turns out to be quite illusory. We subsidise a fleet over the actions of which we are to have no control, and which might sacrifice Sydney to protect Cyprus, according as seemed best for the general defence of the Empire. The Colonies themselves must repel raids on their commercial ports, says the Duke. Which, being so, it may reasonably be asked what are the Colonies paying naval tribute to the Empire for? The raids that we are exposed to are those of Powers which might be at war with England about matters in which the Colonies had no concern. If under these circumstances we hold up our end here by maintaining these ports as a naval base for the Imperial fleets we are doing as much perhaps for the Empire as if we sent our ships to fight in the Yellow Sea or the Bay of Biscay. So that the argument about the Empire battling for us in foreign waters will work as well the other way. The guns on Pinchgut are directed quite as much against the enemies of England as those at any English port are against the enemies of Australia. Surely it is a fair thing, therefore, for England to repel raids on her ports in the same way as the Colonies are asked to do, and not tax us for that purpose.

THE "MELBOURNE ARGUS," *December 10th,* 1896.

As to the employment of the vessels in time of war, that, also, is a matter for the Admiral and the authorities. The enemy that may threaten Australia may best be hit before it reaches Australia. The bold and competent spirits in Elizabeth's day wished to strike at the Armada in the Spanish ports, and theirs were the correct tactics, which England has gloriously adopted on other occasions. In war each situation has to be met as it occurs, but generally the character of the vessels of the Australian squadron indicates what must be the nature of their employment. They are not vessels to fight ironclads or to meet first-class cruisers. But they are sufficiently swift and sufficiently strong to overtake and account for the "sea wolves," who might otherwise do great mischief on the Australian coast. They can establish an effective patrol in the interests of commerce. They can make it difficult for a hostile cruiser to hover unmolested about Cape Howe or Wilson's Promontory or the Otway, setting perhaps forty or fifty vessels ablaze in a day.

The division of responsibility in this matter of defence is easy, and is as the Duke of Devonshire indicates. Great Britain guarantees the Colonies from invasion in force. The Imperial fleet in these waters, with the Australian squadron, acting together, preserve the seas from systematic raiding. And temporary protection from the occasional raider who may escape detection, or from the flying squadron which may effect a *coup*, must be obtained by the local defences which Sydney, Melbourne, and other ports are left to provide for themselves.

THE " MELBOURNE AGE," *December 9th*, 1896.

It is quite reasonable that in the event of a great naval battle being pending in Chinese waters or in the North Pacific the Australian Squadron should be sent to the point of greatest danger, and the Australasian Colonies refrained from any protest when that was first pointed out. But they were bound to have in view the danger to local shipping from an unprotected condition of their coasts. The Colonies had fortified their chief harbours at their own cost, but they had no sea-going force to protect their commerce. It was out of this state of affairs that what is known as the Australasian Agreement between the Colonies and the Mother Country originated. At the joint expense of the Imperial Government and the Australasian Colonies a naval force was to be provided *for the protection of the floating trade in Australasian waters*, without any diminution of the Imperial force. The Imperial Government was to pay the first cost, and the Colonies to pay 5 per cent. on the outlay and the cost of maintenance, not exceeding an annual sum of £91,000. The Imperial authorities gave a generous interpretation to the bargain, and the Colonies have contributed their quota without a murmur.

It is quite true that on occasion it may be advisable to concentrate the British naval forces in the Mediterranean or the English Channel in time of war, leaving the outlying provinces to chance ; but what has that to do with an auxiliary fleet maintained for local purposes by local means? The English critics have obviously misunderstood the position, and so apparently has the President of the Council of Defence.

Colonists must not overlook the fact that a popular project in political circles in the United Kingdom is to get the Colonies in some way or other to contribute to the cost of Imperial defence. At the bottom of the suggestion is the old idea of levying a Colonial tribute. The constitutional position of these Colonies makes it impossible for any such proposal to be acceded to. The cardinal doctrine of the local constitutions, as of that of the Mother Country, is that the control of the expenditure of all moneys raised by taxation shall be vested in the representatives of the taxpayers. This principle would be violated by the handing over to British departments of any portion of the Colonial taxes for the expenditure of which the departments would be responsible only to the representatives of the people of the United Kingdom. It will be remembered that Queensland came very reluctantly into the auxiliary fleet arrangement, and the reason was this very constitutional difficulty.

For Colonies such as ours the natural development is for them to come to the aid of the Mother Country, not by monetary subsidies for defence purposes, but by the gradual provision of defence forces, military and naval, of their own. No objection has been taken to that course in respect to the local land forces and the naval armaments for coast defence. There is no difference in principle between these and a local sea-going fleet. The only practical obstacle has been the absence of a general authority, under which a naval force could be maintained for general purposes. Unfortunately we are not apparently much nearer a Federal Government that we were eight years ago ; but federation is bound to come some day, and it would be unwise to tie the hands of any future Federal Administration by permanent engagements in respect to the defence forces. Although any wide departure from the principles of the existing agreement is not likely to be sanctioned by the Colonies, a revision of details is called for and consequently it is to be presumed there will be no opposition offered to the assembling of a Convention in London next year. ——

THE " BRISBANE COURIER," *December 9th*, 1896.

A general scheme of Imperial defence there must be ; and our Australian Colonies must have part in it. But we are very strongly of opinion that, under the renewed agreement, the part allotted to or accepted by the Colonies should be different from that now existing, under which we are only asked to contribute towards the support of the defending warships.

We are in the position of an unwarlike people which, hopeless itself of acquiring the art of defence, employs mercenaries as its walls. We have spent many thousands of pounds in paying others to protect our ports, and so far as any result in the art of self-protection is concerned, the money might as well have been thrown into the sea. This is what must come to an end. The new agreement must contemplate something more than contributions on the part of the Colonies : it must contemplate action—such action as shall at least make a beginning of self-help. The Duke of Devonshire seemed to have this in mind when he said that the Colonies must be prepared to repel any raids made by hostile cruisers on the commercial ports, as distinct from naval bases. On what scale self-help of this kind should be initiated must be for experts to decide. But a beginning must be made. We must lay the foundation of an Australian Navy which shall be part of the Imperial sea power, not by purchase, but by ships and men.

The weak point in the discussion of this subject as recently cabled to us is its connection. The Duke of Devonshire is addressing the British Empire League, which has made itself obnoxious in its zeal for an entirely different kind of agreement. Not long ago we read how Mr. Lowles, at a meeting of the National Union of Conservative Associations, carried a motion to the amazing effect that the meeting rejoiced to learn that the Australian Colonies favoured the commercial federation of the Empire. Yesterday's cables announced that the National Agricultural Union had passed a resolution establishing a Zollverein or Customs Union between Great Britain and her Colonies, which means that the British farmers' produce is to be protected against all importation except the insignificant fraction which comes from the Colonies. This is after the heart if it is not the direct doing of the British Empire League. At the very meeting addressed by the Duke of Devonshire the representatives of Canada and of New Zealand gleefully anticipated that the difficulties attending a "closer commercial union" with the Colonies would be overcome. Nay, if the Duke is correctly reported, he himself made the surprising assertion that it was unnecessary to approach the Imperial aspects of the British Empire League—that is, those aspects above discussed—until on its commercial side it had proved itself useful in paving the way towards a better understanding between Great Britain and the Colonies. That, if we are to take it as serious, is an ominous pronouncement. It indicates that, so far as the British Empire League and the Duke of Devonshire are concerned, the new naval agreement, if such an agreement as we desire, is to wait upon our acceptance of the League's Commercial Schemes. It seems as if the first was proffered to us by way of a bribe towards the second. On this side of the ocean we are unable to understand how such sentiments or hopes should be expressed or even cherished, except through blinding eagerness to attain the desired object. It is absolutely certain—or as near to absolute certainty as anything human approaches—that the object will never be attained. The Australian Colonies will not consent to it. Britain, sound at heart as ever on Free Trade, will not consent to it. To do so would be to step down from that lofty ideal which the "Spectator" sees realised in Britain's command of the sea, and prostitute it to purely selfish ends. It is genius and enthusiasm worse than wasted. And we protest against the mixing up of so offensive and impracticable a scheme with the large and increasingly important question of the Colonies' development of naval defence.

THE "BALLARAT STAR," *December 8th*, 1896.

The speech of the Duke of Devonshire, President of the British Council of Defence, at the meeting of the British Empire League last week, on the subject of Colonial obligations regarding the defence of the Empire, was timely and appropriate. It may find objectors amongst narrow-minded politicians on both sides of the globe, but patriotic Britons, whether living in the United Kingdom or Australia, will agree with the sentiments expressed. In these Colonies objections to the present arrangement, under which an auxiliary squadron is kept in Australian waters, are urged on two grounds —first, that the fleet protects British commerce and British territory more than it does Australian; and second, that an unfair preference is given to Sydney in making Port Jackson the permanent headquarters of the fleet. The second objection may be brushed aside as too insignificantly parochial for serious consideration, and the first does not merit very much more attention. The simple fact therein stated may be accepted, but the deduction drawn from it is neither logical nor patriotic. It is recognised that, apart from the outlay on the construction of the fleet, its maintenance costs more than £30,000 above what the Colonies contribute. There is also another aspect of the question that must not be forgotten. Battles in defence of Australia's very existence may be more truly fought in the Bay of Biscay, the China Sea, the Indian Ocean, or off the African coast, than in Australian waters. The surest means of defence is, therefore, a mobile fleet, and this is what the Duke of Devonshire insists upon, so that in case of Great Britain being involved in war the auxiliary squadron might sail from these latitudes to fight our battles Armed cruisers would also, in our interests as well as in those of the United Kingdom, patrol the ocean highways to prevent privateering. At present the Colonies pay £126,000 a year for protection against foreign aggression, and it will be admitted by most that this is a very modest insurance premium upon our stationary wealth and floating commerce. On the other hand, it is gratifying to note that the President of the Council of Defence did not take up the tale of those who urge that the Colonies should bear a larger share of the burden of Imperial defence. The dependencies have no voice in determining the foreign policy of the Empire, and while they might be plunged into war without their consent, it is idle to talk of their contributing more liberally to the general defence fund. While the head of the Empire assumes the sole responsibility of ordering foreign affairs, she must be content to bear nearly the whole of the cost of defending her policy. The proposal for the holding of a conference of Colonial and Imperial delegates to consider the whole question of defence is a wise one, and likely to be productive of good. It will probably be preceded by a conference of Colonial Premiers to discuss Australian responsibilities, and at one or the other the key-note of federation may be struck. Never was the necessity for union more urgent, and never were the possibilities of all-round advantage so great as now. All Australians, therefore, will hope that Mr. Reid, the New South Wales Premier, who is on a visit to Queensland, may succeed in arranging with Sir Hugh Nelson a *modus vivendi* by which Queensland may be represented at the proposed Federal Convention next year.

THE "ADVERTISER" (ALBANY, WESTERN AUSTRALIA), *December 10th, 1896.*

The Duke of Devonshire has delivered a very important speech upon the defences of the Empire. He has stated in plain terms that the Mother Country looks to the Colonies to share the cost of their own defence. The claim is a reasonable one, considering the absolute political independence of the Colonies. The various Colonial Governments collect their own revenues and dispense them, and they are free to levy what duties they please. If these Colonies were established on the basis that is adopted with regard to French and German Colonies—the reins of Government being retained by the Mother Country—such a claim as that made by the Duke of Devonshire could not be put forward. Australia will have to continue her contributions to the maintenance of the fleet that protects her shores, and what is more, she will have to strengthen her military forces.

"HOBART MERCURY," *January 9th, 1897.*

The Australasian Colonies have accepted the position, inasmuch as they have contributed towards the squadron now in these waters, but the agreement under which the payments are made will expire shortly, and there should be a clear understanding as to its renewal, whilst some permanent arrangement should be made so as to leave no doubts for the future, and to lay the basis of a permanent arrangement for general defence. This is evidently the next step which requires to be taken, in order that what is now doubtful may be made certain, and the defence of the Empire assume a definite and permanent form. . . . . . . Before these colonies go to another London Conference, they should be able to go, so far as Defence is concerned at least, as one colony. They should be able to say, as it is but a matter of the commonest prudence to be able to say, that they are absolutely united to this end, and that the delegate from any colony can speak in the name of the whole seven. For New Zealand, however much she may object to other forms of Federation, cannot afford to stand out of a union for this purpose, and thus there is a sure prospect of unity, unless, indeed, colonial politicians and the people are lost to all sense of the fitness of things, and to the precautions which are but acts of the commonest prudence. Herein these colonies must act first, and then the Imperial Government may call all the colonies together, and a firm and lasting union for at least one purpose may be made.

THE "NATAL WITNESS," MARTIZBURG, *December 7th*, 1896.

There is still the possibility of some joint action. The time will undoubtedly come when the Colonies will organise local sea forces of their own, just as they now organise local land forces ; and there could be no reason why a Federated Australia should not in a few years have a fleet quite as powerful as that of Austria. There is already the beginning in the vessels for coast defence. If Canada and other groups of Colonies were to do the same and form local fleets, the United Kingdom, in case of war, might be able to rely upon very material aid from such local navies. It will be far better for the Colonies to own and control their own fleets than to send contributions which could be misrepresented as tribute to a central navy, embarrassed and confused by the control of an Imperial Board devoid of cohesion.

THE "NATAL WITNESS," *December 30th*, 1896.

It may not be known to every one that the Imperial Federation League, not having met with the support it expected, resolved about a twelvemonth ago in committing the happy despatch. Shortly afterwards, at the beginning of this year its place was taken by the British Empire League. It was not very much more than a change of name. The principles of the new League are very similar to those of the old. . . . . The meeting was composed of commercial men and citizens

F

ot London. The idea of political union seemed almost inseparable from federation, and that was a reason for the Federation League being dissolved. It has now been determined to try the commercial side. In that way only can Imperial unity, in the opinion of Mr. Chamberlain, be approached. The suggestions in the direction of commercial union at the Ottawa Conference did not offer advantages sufficient to induce Great Britain to incur a certain loss and to take the risk of revising altogether its commercial policy. Lord Ripon, on the eve of quitting office, addressed a despatch to the Colonies, pointing out that there was another proposal involving free trade within the Empire, and that "though it might derogate from the strict principles of free trade," it might be discussed at another Conference. Another will be called at no distant date, as the agreement between the British Government and the Australian Colonies will expire in 1898, which, it is thought, will present a favourable opportunity for opening up the whole question again. The widest proposal of the Ottawa Conference was that differential duties should be imposed in the United Kingdom in favour of colonial produce, and in the Colonies in favour of products of the former. But that involved a reversal of the total trade of the Empire for the advantage and development of a part small by comparison. Lord Ripon said nothing about the chief advantage of the Ottawa proposals— that under a Customs Union colonial trade would be more stable, as it would no longer depend on the whims and fancies of other countries, and would no longer be exposed to the influence of hostile foreign tariffs.

In the opinion of the Imperial Government some naval understanding with the Colonies is a subject of practical and almost immediate importance. The agreement with Australia conceded that the ships of war, the interest on the capital expended and the cost of maintenance being paid by the colonies, should be retained within the limits of the Australian station, and in time of peace are not to be ordered beyond them without the consent of the colonies. That is to be all altered in any future arrangement ; and "to fulfil the great charge"—that is of protection of all the coasts of the Empire— the Government will claim the absolute power of disposing of their forces in the manner they consider most certain to secure success, and object to limit the action of any part of them to the immediate neighbourhood of places which they consider may be more effectively protected by operations at a distance. We should hope that it is generally acknowledged to be the duty of the Imperial Government to afford protection to British subjects, interests, and territory in the event of war, but first to ensure the safety of the head and heart of the Empire, and then to guard all the members. The colonies ought not to be looked to to bear any share of the cost of providing seagoing ships, whether ironclads or unarmoured cruisers ; and it would be most unwise to limit the cruising grounds of such vessels at the request of any Colonial Government, so as to hamper the plans of the Admiral in command, and prevent the concentration of his force for offensive or defensive operations as he may think desirable. The views of the Government will certainly receive the support of the English Press. "We cannot," wrote *The Times* more than a year ago, "give any support whatever to any appeal to colonial sentiment and opinion which is founded, directly or indirectly, on supposed requirements of local defence."

"NATAL MERCURY," *January 7th*, 1897.

The British Empire League, it may be noted, is really the now defunct Imperial Federation League under a different name and a more modest constitution. The new League aims at the absolute unification of the Empire, without committing its members to any particular method of realising the result in view, whereas the Imperial Federation League was considered, at least by many of its members, bound to try and effect union on a fiscal basis. It was the division on this point, in fact, that led to the dissolution of the League in 1893 ; but several of the members recognising that the cause of Imperial unity might suffer, the British Empire League was started to take the place of the Imperial Federation League, but with less ambitious aims and a more modest programme. There were several points in connection with the defunct League on which there was general agreement among the members, chiefly in the matter of a widespread system of Imperial defence, and these points of agreement have been taken as the basis of the constitution of the new League, with the idea that the good and practical work of its predecessor might be continued in a humbler but probably more successful manner, owing to there being less chance of differences of opinion arising on the methods to be pursued and the ultimate aims of the League. The principal speaker at the British Empire League meeting at the Guildhall last month was the Duke of Devonshire, who is President of the League. His speech was an important one, and has attracted a great deal of attention throughout the Empire. . . . . The principles laid down are without doubt sensible and practical, and are also fair and reasonable. No matter how the Navy is, made up, it must be all at the disposal of one responsible head, otherwise there could be no definite plan of action or scheme of defence laid down with any chance of success. It is for the Colonies to say whether they will adopt the recommendations of the Colonial Defence Committee, and agree to the principles laid down as necessary to a complete and secure system of defence throughout the Empire, but the whole scheme is so favourable to the best interests of the Colonies that we hardly imagine there will be the slightest objection raised to co-operating with the Imperial authorities in carrying it out. For the fuller and better discussion of the whole subject, however, a conference to deal solely with the question of Imperial defence and the systems of Imperial communication would be highly useful, and likely to be more fruitful in result than the Imperial conferences where fiscal schemes of unity have largely predominated. The question of a union for purposes of defence involves nothing likely to interfere with the political systems of the various Colonies in the Empire, whereas a commercial union or zollverein raises up conflicting issues of the most vital nature between one Colony and another, and between the Mother Country and her Colonies. The sentiment of unity for self-preservation is universal, and it is quite easy to conceive a system of defence satisfactory to all ; but there are no two countries in the whole Empire with the same ideas as to the best form of commercial union, and there is little chance of any agreement on that subject for a very long time to come. The British Empire League intends to devote itself to such matters as Imperial defence, with the hope that by attaining unity in such a matter the way may be paved to unity in other directions, all tending towards the cultivation of a desire towards the complete unification of the Empire in all that is embodied in the phrase,

"Unity is strength." There is no disunion between England and her Colonies just now—indeed, the ties binding them were never closer—but in many ways there could be closer union, and chiefly in the matter of a joint system of defence. If the British Empire League helps this forward, it will be doing a noble work, and will in every sense justify its existence.

"PORT ELIZABETH TELEGRAPH," *January* 5*th*, 1897.

In Great Britain the Imperial spirit is constantly making itself felt in the formation of Leagues or Unions, whose object it is to maintain the unity of the Empire and to organise it on proper lines. The present is a stage of transition from the exploded notions of colonial independence to the untried devices of Imperial Federalism, and these leagues serve the useful purpose of keeping up public attention to the subject, and of familiarising men's minds with the various suggestions which have been made for the organisation of the Empire. The latest outcome of this yearning for national unity has been the formation of an organisation known as "The British Empire League." A meeting of this body was recently held at the Guildhall, at which the Lord Mayor was in the chair and the Duke of Devonshire was the principal speaker. The latter bore witness to the progress which the Imperial sentiment was making among all sorts and conditions of men at home and abroad, but he regretted the occurrence of certain checks and disappointments as regards the practical realisation of ideas. Among other failures he referred to the dissolution of the Imperial Federation League. . . . . In fact, the British Empire League has been formed for the purpose of entering into the labours of the Imperial Federation League at the point where the later organisation ceased them, and that it was proposed "to continue the operations of its predecessor in respect of informing and educating the public mind." The Duke of Devonshire agreed with Mr. Chamberlain in urging that Imperial unity must be approached on its commercial side, and pleaded that Mr. Chamberlain had done no more than Lord Ripon in urging that a plan of free trade within the Empire would be a legitimate subject for discussion at another Colonial Conference. The Duke of Devonshire made an interesting remark with reference to the naval agreement with the Australian Colonies. The idea has got abroad that this agreement was not on the whole a satisfactory one, but his statement that the Government set the greatest value on its renewal will reassure the public mind. The Duke further hoped that the Colonies would readily adopt the recommendations of the Government's Colonial Defence Committee, which, he stated, assigned to the Colonies a very moderate share in the work of defence. We have no doubt that the various Governments will give favourable consideration to their recommendations. It is rumoured that our own Government has pledged itself to the expenses of coast defence on a fairly large scale, and no one can desire to criticise such action. In fact, the South African coast has been shamefully neglected in times past, and large sums of money have been squandered upon Table Bay and its neighbourhood, to the neglect of every other place. The scheme includes the defence of Port Elizabeth and East London, and it certainly is high time that the work were undertaken. In the discussion which followed the Duke of Devonshire's speech reference was made to the fact that the purchase of British goods by the inhabitants of the Colonies is many times greater per head of the population than the purchase of such goods by foreigners. Sir Charles Tupper pointed out that whereas the self-governing Colonies took of British products 51s. 8d. per head, the United States took only 6s. and the German 7s. 2d. per head. But it must not be forgotten that though the United States takes per head only one-seventh of the amount taken by the Colonies, its population is at least seven times as great as all the European Colonies put together. The moral of these figures is not that Great Britain should take any steps which would be calculated to discourage trade with the United States, but should rather systematically encourage emigration to the British Colonies, where the emigrants become such valuable customers. Another point which must be considered in reference to these figures, and figures such as these, is the fact that as manufactures grow in the Colonies, and as mineral wealth is developed in them, the tendency to look to England for supplies must to some extent diminish. How gravely, for example, the discovery of coal in the Stormberg and in Natal has reduced our need to look to England for our supply. We have every good wish for such organisations as the British

Empire League. Their meetings and discussions are the true solvents of many erroneous notions which still prevail with reference to the relation of the dependencies to the Mother Country. Men of the Colonies, and men who have not travelled, meet on a common platform for their mutual benefit. We believe that men like the Duke of Devonshire, who are only conservative in a restricted way, are never better employed than when they are endeavouring to devise a plan whereby a new form may be given to the old relations of the Parliament at Westminster with the other Parliaments which represent Greater Britain in various quarters of the world.

THE " VICTORIA COLONIST," B.C., *December 29th*, 1896.

COLONIES AND THE EMPIRE.—" Defence not defiance," was, it may be remarked, the keynote of the gathering, the object of all present, and all who sympathise with the movement, being the consolidation of British prowess and British institutions, as embodied in the Empire, and the intensification of the feeling that colonists as well as natives of the Islands are heirs of all the ages in the almost boundless march of time as concerns the progress, the greatness, the power and the influence for good of all that may be claimed to be British.

" LONDON (ONTARIO) FREE PRESS," *December 7th*, 1896.

IMPERIAL DEFENCE.—It is understood that the Canadian Government will cordially co-operate, so far as its means will allow, in the great scheme of Imperial defence which the Duke of Devonshire, speaking for the British Ministry, elaborated before the British Empire League on Thursday. Australian assent is equally sure. For the first time England formally accepts the responsibility of protecting her colonies against an organised invasion from the sea. Canada and South Africa have been asked to follow Australia's example and provide colonial squadrons to protect the colonies from the casual raids of chance cruisers, but in future these squadrons will be under the entire control of the British Admiralty, not, as is the case with the Australian squadron, confined to colonial waters. England continues to defend places like Halifax and Esquimalt, which are essential to her navy force coaling, refitting and repairing. The colonies are expected to make adequate defence at such places as Quebec, Montreal, Niagara and Vancouver, and to bring the colonial forces up to the required British standard. This scheme is England's first move towards Imperial federation. Mr. Chamberlain's idea of federation through customs houses was calmly put aside by the Duke of Devonshire as not even a fit subject for another colonial conference.

———◆

"THE MONTREAL GAZETTE," *January 18th*, 1897.

The Duke of Devonshire, as chairman of the Cabinet Committee on Defence, recently took the public into the confidence of the Government, and laid before them an "authorized scheme" of defence, which has perhaps hardly attracted so much attention in Canada as it deserves. Sir Charles Tupper refers to it in an interesting interview published in another part of this issue, and has assured the British public of Canada's willingness to do her share. The main idea of the scheme is that the mother country undertakes the entire responsibility for maintaining British supremacy at sea and protecting the whole of the Empire against organized invasion from the sea, while the colonies are expected to look after their own local defences. "Generally speaking," says an article in the London *Times*, which seems to be written from inside knowledge, "the precautions called for are neither very extensive nor very costly. They amount usually to such preparations as will suffice to repel a sudden attack by an enemy's cruiser which may elude the utmost vigilance of the most powerful fleet." The Colonial Defence Committee of the Cabinet, of which the Duke of Devonshire is chairman, has gone carefully into the question from the point of view of each particular colony, and, with the assistance of its naval and military advisers, has defined the kind and degree of local defence which each colony ought to provide and the attacks to which they may be subject short of great movements, against which the Imperial Govenment will take precautions. This information has been confidentially communicated to the Dominion Cabinet, and has doubtless received their most serious consideration. But as to the leading features of the scheme, the Canadian public have been taken into the confidence of the Imperial Government, and may

reasonably be expected to take an interest in the matter, for it is
their money which is being spent, and their homes which are
being protected.

THE "TIMES OF INDIA," *December 28th*, 1896.

IMPERIAL DEFENCE.—The Continental journals regard the
Duke of Devonshire's speech at the Guildhall as containing the
most important declaration made by ministers since their
accession to office. As chairman of the Defence Committee of
the Cabinet, the Duke stated that the maintenance of sea
supremacy has been taken as the basis of the system of imperial
defence against attack from the sea. The whole defensive
policy of Britain and her Colonies is the establishment and
maintenance of the command of the seas ; and the Admiralty
undertake to protect all British territory abroad against
organised invasion from the sea. The Duke not merely
intimated to our friends and rivals that in the event of war
breaking out the naval policy of England to-day is identical
with that of 1805 ; he revealed that ports have been selected
which are to be made "absolutely secure" for the purpose of
enabling the Navy to coal, refit, and repair vessels of war ;
and the Colonies are now expected to provide for their own land
defences.

THE "CALCUTTA STATESMAN," *December 24th*, 1896.

If the British Empire League will honestly discard Jingoism
and proceed on business lines, it may, as is pointed out by a
critic, escape the fate of its parent, the now defunct Imperial
Federation League. The remarks of the Duke of Devonshire
left nothing to desire on this score. He has no enthusiasms,
and is therefore the best President the new League could have
got. His speech might have been delivered at the annual
meeting of a joint-stock company. The Colonists will appre-
ciate its practical commonsense. They are not to be caught by
claptrap, but are ready to listen to business-like proposals.

G

LONDON :

SPOTTISWOODE AND CO., PRINTERS,

54 GRACECHURCH STREET E.C.

The Secretary,

BRITISH EMPIRE LEAGUE,

BOTOLPH HOUSE, EASTCHEAP, E.C.

Please enrol my name as a Member of the "BRITISH EMPIRE LEAGUE." *which I intend to subscribe annually to*

I enclose herewith £   :   :   the funds of the League.

NAME

ADDRESS ....

CHEQUES SHOULD BE CROSSED "ROBARTS, LUBBOCK & CO."

TERMS OF MEMBERSHIP.

Minimum Subscription of Membership One Guinea per annum.

The Friends of the League are reminded of the great expense necessarily incurred in the production and in the distribution, under the existing postal system, of its correspondence and literature.

Subscriptions in excess of the above towards meeting this expenditure will be gladly received and acknowledged by the Secretary.

www.ingramcontent.com/pod-product-compliance
Lightning Source LLC
Chambersburg PA
CBHW031445270326
41930CB00007B/877